Beyond the Pale

Matthew Turner effectively turns our collective struggles into a meaningful story to help us all navigate some of our eternal questions with a bit more perspective, humility, and hope. We need new definitions of success in our world and this book helps us ask the right questions to get there.

Houston Kraft, author of Deep Kindness,
and co-founder of CharacterStrong

What does it mean to truly succeed? Through this deep and reflective business fable, Matthew Turner asks us to explore what matters most, and how we measure our business and our lives.

Dorie Clark, bestselling author of *Entrepreneurial You*,
and executive education faculty, Duke University
Fuqua School of Business

I'm a big fan of the business fable format - it's engaging, interesting, and lets us internalize important messages through story - the medium that our brains are wired to most easily comprehend.

Danny Iny, bestselling author of *Teach Your Gift* and *Teach and Growth Rich*, and founder/CEO at Mirasee

Matthew Turner makes you reflect differently about the big picture - purpose, passion, hustle, flow, the different perspectives of consciousness. *Beyond the Pale* is that business fable, the one you focus, ponder, and happily lose sleep over, then go around urging all your colleagues to read.

Richie Norton, bestselling author of
The Power of Starting Something Stupid

Entrepreneur and author Matthew Turner authentically captures the desires, dreams, and cost of "the hustle" in *Beyond the Pale*.

Tom Morkes, author of *Collaborate*, and founder
of Insurgent Publishing

Through *Beyond the Pale*, Matthew Turner provides Important lessons into what true success and fulfillment is all about.

Erlend Bakke, bestselling author of *Never Work Again*, and Serial Entrepreneur

Embraced by the muses - *Beyond the Pale* is filled with empowering stories of wisdom and awareness that will inspire you to trust that there's always hope, even in the most difficult times. This book will guide you in living your greatest life, ensuring you make the most out the 'one life' you are given.

Leonard Kim, author of *Ditch The Act*

A parable for modern times. The journey of discovery that Ferdinand embarks on takes the reader on their own voyage, inviting self-reflection and increased awareness of our own aspirations and the future we are working towards.

Andy Lopata, author of *Just Ask*, and Professional Relationships Strategist

A reflective, creative approach to exploring the definition of success in business and life. Matthew Turner's ability to share stories is brilliant and shows the balance of hard work and flow for the millennial entrepreneur.

Adam Smith, author of *The Bravest You*

If you want to live a bigger story, read this book. That's the gift of Beyond the Pale, a business fable for modern times. The stories you choose make the world.

Michael Margolis, author of *Story 10x: Turn the Impossible Into the Inevitable*,and founder/CEO at Storied

Spur greater and uplifting success in your work via this uplifting, engrossing fable about how Ferdinand did that in this engrossing book, *Beyond the Pale*, by my widely admired friend, Matthew Turner.

Kare Anderson, author of *Mutuality Matters* and popular TED Talk *Opportunity Makers*

Matthew Turner is a master storyteller! *Beyond the Pale* gives us a compass for regaining control over our lives. I recommend this book to anyone who is ready and willing to take full responsibility for themselves and the destiny of both your business and personal life.

Ari Meisel, author of *The Art of Less Doing*, and founder of Less Doing

BEYOND THE PALE

A Fable about ESCAPING *the* HUSTLE *and* FINDING YOURSELF

MATTHEW TURNER

NEW YORK

LONDON • NASHVILLE • MELBOURNE • VANCOUVER

BEYOND THE PALE

A Fable about ESCAPING *the* HUSTLE *and* FINDING YOURSELF

Published in New York, New York, by Morgan James Publishing. Morgan James is a trademark of Morgan James, LLC. www.MorganJamesPublishing.com

ISBN 9781631953842 paperback
ISBN 9781631953859 eBook
Library of Congress Control Number: 2020948952

Cover and Interior Design by:
Chris Treccani
www.3dogcreative.net

To George and Imogen, my inspiration, always.

ACKNOWLEDGMENTS

Writing a book is always a journey. Much of it takes place within, but a great deal involves other people. Some of these kind individuals help in a literal sense, such as my talented editors, Joe and Rea, and David and the team at Morgan James Publishing. You all helped make this book what it is, and I tip my cap to you all.

Other folk help in a less literal way, offering support, wisdom, and an ever-necessary shoulder to lean on. To my family, friends, mentors, and peers, thank you. You know who you are, and I hope you appreciate the incredible role you play, not only in my writing but life as a whole.

Finally, I cannot end without thanking those who appear in the book—the ones I sat down with and spoke to and who allowed me to place them amongst Ferdinand's adventure. Jordan, AJ, Matt, Ishita, Kamal, Gini, Hollis, Jules, Michael, and Sol . . . thank you.

And to you, the person reading this, thank you. I'm always amazed at the notion there are people who sit down and lose themselves among the words I once wrote. May this particular book keep you company, and inspire you to venture beyond your own pale.

ONE.

Coi Restaurant, San Francisco

She spins her spoon on the table, lips pouting and her head slightly shaking from side to side. I hold the phone to my ear, listening but not. I hear the words and passively take them in after another day of endless meetings.

"Okay," I say. "Sure. We can talk more about it next week." Still, the words keep flowing, me nodding and motioning my hand in a circle. "Okay. Okay. I've got to go. Thanks." I place the phone in my pocket. "Sorry about that," I say, moving my hand to the middle of the table. "Where were we?"

"I think it's time, Ferdinand," she says, clearing her throat and stopping the spoon mid-spin. She avoids looking at me, her eyes dancing from the entrance to the kitchen, to other tables and above my head.

"Time for what?"

Closing her eyes, she sighs. "Us."

"Us? What about us, Beckie?"

She looks at me finally. "Come on, you know," she says with a half-smile. It was the first thing I noticed when I approached her in the bar. *When was it, exactly? Eighteen months ago?* She had flashed me that half-smile as I tried to buy her a drink. I knew straight away it would take a lot more than one drink to get her to let her guard down.

I shrug.

She laughs, effortlessly, as she does so often, accompanying her half-smile. "In fact, that makes sense," she says. "I imagine no girl has ever dared break up with you."

"You're breaking up with me?" I ask quietly, observing our surroundings and noticing how close our fellow diners are to us. Small wooden tables barely a foot apart, a fluffy white cushion the only barrier between Beckie and the women next to her. "Where's this coming from?" I ask, a little louder. "We were just enjoying an amazing meal and this wine," I continue, picking up the glass. "The best wine we've had in a long time."

"Yeah. It is. And that's the problem."

"I don't understand."

With a long sigh, she places her napkin on the table and leans toward me. "You canceled this dinner three times already. You've been out past eleven each day this week. Have you even noticed that I haven't been staying at your place for the last two weeks?"

"What do you mean not staying at mine? Sure you have."

"No, Ferdinand, I haven't. Not that your place is mine. We've only been dating for two years, but have you asked me to move in? No. Do we ever talk about the future?"

"Of course we do. We were talking about the future just earlier."

She laughs. Not the effortless kind this time, either. "You were talking about your business's future. You always talk about the future of Contollo and your future as some rock star CEO, but we never talk about *our* future. And you never ask me about mine."

"Well, I always figured your future was the same as mine. You're part of my future, Beckie. I love you."

Rubbing her eyes, she shakes her head. "No, you don't, Ferdinand." A waiter walks past our table, disturbing the tablecloth as he does. The room's perfectly lit, not too bright but far from dark. A long, slim painting rests above Beckie's head, an assortment of white circles and swirls on a dark black canvas. "I don't think you even know what love is," she continues. "I'd say you love yourself, but I'm not even sure about that anymore. I'd say you love your business and your amazing career and everything that it offers, but again, I'm not sure that is true."

"Come on," I say, holding up my hands. "I love you. I love my business, and I love my life. I love our life together, and I thought you did, too."

"So this comes as a surprise to you?"

"Yes. This is completely out of the blue."

She slumps back into her chair, her eyes tightening and glistening in the light. "That's really sad, Ferdinand. It's sad that you haven't noticed any of this. You don't notice me. You don't see that I'm unhappy. You don't even notice if I'm there or not . . ."

Silence falls over us as the chatter around from other tables takes over. Couples laughing and sharing stories. Work colleagues having fun, clinking glasses, and letting off steam. An older couple to the right of us, holding hands over their empty plates.

"But, what?"

"I don't know," she says. "I know you're not a bad person, but these days I'm not sure what kind of person you are. You've always been busy. You've always had ambition. It's one of the things that first attracted me to you. You were passionate. If something was important to you, you were all in. But over the last year, you have . . . I don't know. Changed."

"Changed? I haven't changed. I'm the same person I've always been. You knew what you signed up for when you agreed to date me."

"What I signed up for?" she asks, incredulous. "When I *agreed* to date you? Ferdinand, do you hear yourself? I'm not one of your employees. I didn't sign up for anything, and I didn't agree to date you. We met, and I liked you, and I liked us, and we lived life with each other. For a time, I thought I would live the rest of my life with you. But I've known that isn't the case for some time now."

"Where is this coming from?"

"Haven't you heard anything I've just said?"

"Yeah, sure, but—" I take a deep breath, close my eyes, and try to clear my head. "Look, I know it's been a crazy year. With the big round of investment and, well, you know what it's like. We're growing exponentially. It's a busy time, but it will even out over the next few months."

"Will it?"

"I promise."

"I'm sure you believe that's true," she says. "But it isn't. You're not busy because you're always working. It's not like you're in the office until midnight every day. Your life is spent in meetings, and then you just hang out with your minions most nights at some club or an event that you just *have* to attend."

"That's part of work, Beckie."

"If that's what you tell yourself."

"It is."

"Fine. Well, if that is true, you've confirmed all my suspicions."

"What?"

"Like, you don't care about me. At least, you don't care about me enough to have me as a priority in your life. Be honest, do I even make the top five?"

"Of course you do."

She raises her brow.

"You are. We're here, aren't we? We've had a nice evening, right?"

She nods. "But one evening every couple of weeks isn't a relationship. We've been dating over two years. How did we spend our anniversary?"

I freeze. "I . . .We . . . It was . . ."

"We did nothing, Ferdinand. For weeks, I kept asking you about it. I spoke to Christian, to make sure he put it in your precious calendar and to remind you. Which, he did. He even booked us at Quince and arranged a weekend away in Big Sur. But you canceled both because 'something came up.'"

I look away and down at my empty wine glass.

"What's worse, you didn't even cancel. You had Christian do it. You never even spoke to me about it afterwards. It's like it never happened. In your head, maybe it didn't."

"Okay. I'm sorry. And you're right. I have been . . ." I pause. "You're right. I'm sorry."

"It's fine. I'm over it. I've been over it for a while. I tried to make it work, and I tried to talk to you about it. I tried to give you space because I know this last year has been tough. And I hoped it would get better once you closed your precious deal, but I kinda always knew it wouldn't change anything. And it hasn't."

"It will change, though. I will change. I've heard you, and I see where you're coming from, and—"

She reaches out and takes my hand. "It's over, Ferdinand. I loved you. And I leave this with some great memories. I hope you do, too. But I don't love you anymore. Not like that. I don't hate you, but if I don't walk away now, I'm afraid I might."

I remove my hand and place both of them on my knees, straightening my back and puffing out my cheeks. "So, that's it? No second chance? No conversation?"

"Don't."

"Don't, what?"

"Don't try and make out that this is out of the blue. Just because you've been too oblivious to notice, doesn't mean that it hasn't been a long time coming. If you spend just a few minutes outside of *Ferdinand Land*, I think you'll see that."

"Hey, come on—"

"Don't," she interrupts, her tone stern.

"Fine," I say, biting my lip and taking another deep breath. "So, where do we go from here?"

"Nothing changes for you," she says. "I've already moved the few things you allowed me to have in your house, and next week I'm heading back to stay with my parents for a while."

"You're going back to Michigan?"

"There's nothing keeping me here. I came to start a career, but then I met you, and everything got put on hold. I'm not even sure what I want to do anymore. But I'm certain whatever it is, it isn't in a city like this."

"What's wrong with San Francisco?"

She sighs. "Everything."

"It's one revelation after another tonight."

"It really isn't, Ferdinand. But the fact you think it is says everything." She finishes her wine and pushes out her chair, rising to her feet and brushing down her long, elegant, black dress. Her wavy, blonde hair catches the light, her blue eyes standing out as they do in a gently lit setting like this. It was that smile that pulled me, but it was those eyes that captured my attention in the first place.

"I don't want things to be strange between us," she says. "In time, I would like us to be friends. If you want that, too. But right now, please, just don't call me."

"What, so I'm not allowed to fight for you?"

"I don't want you to. I've thought through this a lot, trust me. I'm hurting." She pauses, shuts her eyes. "You've hurt me, Ferdinand. I've been hurt for a while, and I just want to get away from all this and not hurt anymore. Please, let me do that." Her eyes glisten in the light again. "Please."

My chest aches as my heart races, realizing this may be the final time I see those eyes; the blue tainted red, shaking from the threat of tears.

"Okay," I say quietly.

"Thank you." She raises her shoulders and brushes down her dress once more before forcing a smile. "Good-bye, Ferdinand."

I watch her walk away, her long legs effortlessly taking her to the door, and, then, in an instant, out of it. A rush of fresh, cool air replaces her, flowing over the table and onto my face. I'm alone, two empty plates with matching empty glasses, discarded napkins, and splatters of sauce across the crisp, white tablecloth.

The chatter around me grows in volume, colleagues laughing, couples talking, waiters taking orders, and the barman crunching ice. It's a wall of sound, nothing clear enough to make out. Just noise. Just other people's noise, and me, here, stuck in silence. I reach for my wine glass but remember it's empty. The water glass is, too. There is nothing to consume but my own thoughts.

It feels like butterflies flutter inside me, working their way around my stomach and chest, along each arm and down both legs. I close my eyes and breathe to slow down my racing heart, gather my thoughts, and collect some sense of control. I'm used to slowing it all down like this. The endless meetings and unpredictable conversations.

I've been here before. Breathe. Just breathe. Open your eyes. Gather yourself. Be strong. Look in control.

"Can I get you anything else, Mr. Foy?" The waiter asks, approaching the table.

"No. Thank you. Here," I say, rooting into my jacket pocket and handing over my card. "I need to get going. Can you arrange a car for me?"

"Of course." He nods and walks away, back toward the bar where the barman continues crunching ice.

"Geez," I whisper. "Where did all that come from?"

It's been a busy year, and at times, I imagine, I'm not the easiest person to be in a relationship with. But who is? In a position like mine? I treated her well. We've gone on amazing vacations. We've had fun. What more can she expect at a time like this when I'm building something so important?

I sigh, rubbing my eyes and picturing her face, not the one that's just departed, but rather the version with that smile, cheek-to-cheek. The way she would stare at me and blink slowly, brushing her hair behind her ear before gently biting her lip.

"All sorted, Mr. Foy," says the waiter. "Your car is waiting outside, whenever you're ready."

I nod and retrieve my card from the table, push it into my pocket, and rise to my feet. "I don't have time for this," I mutter, heading toward the door. "I will be just fine. In fact, it will be better this way."

Pulling the door open, I head out and into the night air, cooler but still warm. The evening is young, and I now have the time to enjoy it.

TWO.

In a Private Car, San Francisco

The glass is cool on my forehead as I stare out of the window, the final remnant of light clinging to San Francisco's skyline. There's an entire night of darkness ahead, and now I get to enjoy it in a place where opportunity meets excitement. I always meet the most interesting people on nights like this. This is how someone like me should be spending his time, not at home watching a movie or drinking wine around a pool.

Nobody builds an empire that way.

I pull my phone out of my pocket, bring the screen to life, and take note of the numbers that greet me, letting me know of all the unread messages, texts, emails, replies, and voicemails I have. The numbers never fall, only rise. No time to face them, not now. I open my contacts—type *Christian*, click call, and hold the phone up to my ear. He'll know where I should go tonight.

"Hey, Ferdinand," he says, picking up on the fourth ring. "How's dinner?"

"Don't get me started."

"Why, what happened?"

"Nothing. It's fine. Beckie and me, though, we're past tense."

"Wait, really? Why?"

"I don't know. Totally out of the blue if you ask me, but apparently, she's not been happy for a while. She seemed more than happy enjoying all the stuff I bought her, but not now that I have to work late some of the time, and, you know, run a successful business."

"Man, sorry to hear that. You okay?"

"Yeah. I'm fine. It's not like we were going to get married. Plus, it's been two years. A good time to move on for both of us."

"I guess," he says. "But still kind of sucks. You were good together."

"You think?"

"Yeah. I liked Beckie. She was good for you."

I picture her face again, those eyes looking at me, this time red and stained, glistening in the light.

"Whatever. It's done. Time to move on."

"Okay. Well, if you say—"

"So here's the thing," I say, cutting him off. "I now have an entire night to enjoy, but I'm not sure where the best place to go is. I've just told the driver to drive around for a while. So, the man who knows more about my life than I do . . . where should I go tonight?"

"Tonight? What were you thinking?"

"I'm open to whatever, so long as it has alcohol. On a night like this, the older the whiskey, the better."

"Well, there's an event at Gallery 308. Sasha's running it."

"Perfect. Can you call ahead, and let her know that I'm coming."

"Yeah. But are you sure you want to? I can come over, if you want, and talk. I imagine you want to get a few things off your chest."

"Nope. I'm good."

"Okay. If you're sure—"

"I am."

"Well, don't drink too much. You have a stacked day tomorrow."

"Like every other day, then," I say. "Okay, so hit me. What's on the agenda for tomorrow? When do I start?"

"Your first call is at seven, and you're back-to-back until eleven," he says. "So the good news is you don't have to leave the house until then, but you need to get to Union Street at noon, and—"

"What's that for?"

"The podcast with Jordan Harbinger. Dorie set it up."

"Oh, yeah. What about the afternoon?" I ask.

"A few meetings at the office, and you have dinner with Ray and drinks with—"

"Okay, okay. You're sending all this over to me in a message, right?"

"Yes."

"Good. Do me a favor and keep some time free in the evening. If I know Sasha, I'll meet some interesting people tonight so may have a last minute meeting or two to set up."

"Okay, I'll make a few adjustments," he says, a clicking sound of his keyboard accompanies his words.

"Hold on a second." I lean toward the driver and move my hand into his eye line. "Can you take me to Gallery 308 at Fort Mason?" I ask, then settle back in my seat and hold the phone to my ear. "Okay, so just internal meetings tomorrow, right?"

"Yeah. Other than that interview, it's all internal. It's a busy day, though. You're back-to-back until . . ." he pauses. "Ten, maybe even eleven at night."

"The way I like it," I say, smiling. "Plus, nobody to distract me now."

"Yeah." Christian pauses again. "You know, it's okay if you do want to talk about anything. You and Beckie have been dating for over two years. It's a long time, so if you want to talk about, you know, anything . . . we can."

"I appreciate it, Christian. But I'm fine. Seriously, it's probably a long time coming. Like I said, we were never going to get married, and come on, if we did, it would only get messy. How many people in a situation like mine end up getting divorced? I don't need anything like that, so her leaving now is a blessing."

"Okay. If you say so. I guess I'll let you go. I'll call Sasha. You know where to find me if you need me."

"Have a good night, Christian."

I place the phone into my pocket and lean back, looking out at the passing buildings and lit streetlights. I close my eyes for a second and it hits me—how tired I am. These last few weeks have been hectic. In fact, these last few months have been constant. One opportunity followed by another. It feels only moments ago since we brought in the New Year.

The first time I met Beckie like yesterday.

I picture her face again, that half-smile and how it instantly had me the first time we met. A night not all dissimilar to this one. A day of meetings followed by an evening of events and drinks with potential investors. I didn't plan to go out that night, just as I didn't plan to go out now. A quick escape before another day of back-to-backs, and there she was, alone at the bar as she waited for her friends. Her red dress, long, bare legs, and slightly curled blonde hair. Those blue eyes that seemed painted on in the bright, fluorescent lighting from the bar. Just another girl, but at the same time, not. Before I even approached her, my chest fluttered. I remember feeling so tired, yet given a new sense of energy the moment I laid eyes on her. It feels like yesterday. But the two years since? I can barely comprehend how so much time has passed.

I sigh, forcing her face out of my thoughts.

"For the best," I say under my breath.

I smile over this now spontaneous night where so much could happen. Sasha always throws the best events. I was going to miss it, but now I won't. Who knows who I'll meet. Who knows what will happen over the next few hours.

"Hey," I say to the driver. "Do you have anything up there with caffeine in it?"

He holds up a bright blue can. "I have this," he says. "Tastes awful but packs a punch."

"Sounds perfect." I take it from him and force my nail under the tab, pulling up until I feel the fizz vibrate against my finger. I take a sip, wincing as it touches my tongue. "What flavor is this?"

"I don't think it's a flavor. Just chemicals and sugar. It works, though. I always drink it when I drive through the night."

I purse my lips and scrunch up my nose. "Well, here goes nothing," I say, downing the can's content as it burns its way down my throat and into my stomach. "That is," I hold my hand to my mouth, "terrible. That may be the most awful thing I've ever tasted."

The driver laughs. "Yep. The good news is you won't have to sleep for the next two days."

"That is good," I say, more to myself than to him. "I have no time to sleep."

I lean back and pull out my phone, although I'm not sure why. A screen of notifications greets me once more, the numbers higher than earlier, and I have neither the time nor motivation to open any of the apps and face what's inside. Instead, I launch my camera, hold my phone out as far as I can reach, smile, and click. Inspecting the photo, I swipe left and consider each filter and hue available, settle on one, swipe again, click, and send it to an app and begin typing. It's all automatic, fingers forming words and hashtags. Pressing send, I wait a second, and there. Just like that, I've published across the world to my two million followers.

This time last year, it was less than half of that. This time next year, it will be many millions more.

I swipe down and refresh the screen, already hundreds of likes and dozens of comments. I smile, although not sure why. It means nothing. I know it doesn't, but . . .

I sigh, push my phone in my pocket and rub both my cheeks. "I just need a few drinks," I whisper. "Just need to let go a little and have a good night."

I look out of the window again, cars rushing past in the opposite direction, blurs of light as night has almost completely set in. I press the little button and watch as the window slips down and welcomes a rush of air into my face, cooling my eyes and forehead. Taking a deep breath of the fresh air in, I hold it in my lungs. I feel the toxic energy from the drink coarse through me, my fingers tensing and my legs growing restless. Yet my mind remains unaffected, lethargic, and tempting me to close my eyes.

Not now. Wake up. A few drinks will make it better.

My leg vibrates—a new message to my phone. I slip it out, glad for the distraction.

I'll meet you at the entrance xx, it says, from Sasha. I smile. Soon, my night can begin.

THREE.

Temple Night Club, San Francisco

The bass trembles through my feet, rising up my legs and tickling my thighs, then running up my spine to my neck, my ears hearing, as well as feeling, the sound come through me. The incessant beats have me in a trance, although the five—*or is it six?*—drinks may be playing a role.

Sasha's event, as they always are, was a hit. A launch party for some new drink company, full of beautiful people—some I knew, many that I didn't. Models painted from head-to-toe, sharing drinks and posing for pictures. Other models on stilts, walking around and handing out food. I've already forgotten the name of the brand, but if Sasha has anything to do with it, it will become well known soon enough. A few of us left before the party grew stale, filing into Temple before getting ushered into the VIP area, a roped off private booth that's literally at the center of the room.

I remember a time when I used to laugh at people who sat in supposedly private areas like this, paying stupid amounts of money for the privilege. Private and out of the way of everyone else, yet in the midst of them so they can see what they're missing. Part of the same floor or the same room, nothing but a velvet rope standing between those inside and those out. I guess I laughed at people like that because I wanted to be like them. I didn't want to sit on the outside, looking in with envy, curious about what it'd be like to be in there. I wanted to be the one surrounded by the rope, a bottle to myself, and the freedom to pour as much as I want, when I want. No permission. No limitation.

"Great night, huh?" Sasha says, sitting beside me.

I nod. "You always put on a great show."

She smiles, raising her glass and clinking it into mine. Leaning closer, she practically shouts into my ear. "Where's Beckie?"

I hold in a breath, reminded of why I'm here in the first place. "We broke up."

She looks at me, surprise filling her eyes. "When did this happen?"

"Earlier tonight."

"Sorry, dude," she says, placing her hand on my shoulder. "You okay?"

"I'm fine. It's been coming."

She nods, finishing her drink and placing the glass on the table. "A good excuse to get another bottle sent to the table," she says. "In fact, how about we go all out?" Picking up the drinks menu, she points to the last item on the list. "What do you say? A bottle of Johnnie Walker Blue?"

I smile. "Sure," I say, recalling how I used to also laugh at the fact that a bottle with such a price tag existed, assuming anyone who ordered it to be insane. Sasha walks toward the rope and wraps her arm around a waitress, pointing to the menu, smiling and shaking her hips. She owns an area like this, moving from person to person, spending just enough time with everyone to remain top of their minds. Always dancing. Always moving. Always grinning, laughing, flirting.

She moves over to Joe, hugs him and takes his drink, sips from it. I don't know Joe's last name, although I've known him for three years. This is the third time I've partied with him this week, a fellow entrepreneur with his own thriving business. He faces Tori, a model who posts makeup tutorials to a million-plus subscribers, and also Seth, a former football player who's now a personal trainer to wealthy executives. We all know the same people. We all go to the same places and follow each other online. We're all friends, although sometimes it feels like it's in name only. It's one of the reasons I've spent so many of these nights alone. Beckie never enjoyed life behind the rope.

"There's just no substance to anything," she'd say. "Everyone talks about the same thing, boasting about their latest success and gloating about who they met on their trip to Bali last month. I honestly cannot remember a single conversation I've enjoyed with any of them. Can you?"

"They're fine," I had replied. "It's just part of the scene. We all do business with each other and know the same people. It's how I've met just about every one of my investors."

I picture her face again, red-eyed and sad, the moment before she left the restaurant. She will already be in bed. She no longer has to pretend to enjoy nights like this or spending time with these people, no longer has to pretend to love me. I sigh. She never understood. She's never appreciated what it takes to build something important in a city like this.

"I hear you and Beckie broke up," says Joe, snapping me back. "You okay, brother?"

"I'm fine. We just wanted different things in life. No big deal."

"I'll drink to that," he says, raising his glass. "It's hard to find a girl who gets what we do."

I nod. "How's business?"

"Good." He smiles. "We should grab lunch soon. I'm working on something big that you'll love."

"Sounds good. You have Christian's number, right?"

"I do. I'll set it up." He sits beside me, crosses his legs, and leans back. "You know who I was thinking of the other day? Wil. What happened to that crazy mother?"

"He moved east to Ohio or something."

"Ohio? Why in the world would he move there?"

"I don't know. I haven't spoken to him for a while. He's kinda dropped off the radar."

"Man, that's crazy. He was always out. That guy would have me laughing for hours, talking about the most random things." He downs his drink and plants his hand on my thigh. "Good speaking to you, Ferdinand. I'll set up that lunch. You're gonna love what we're doing."

I move to reply, but he's gone before I get a chance. Sipping from my glass, the smooth whiskey slips down my throat, soothing, as my head tingles from the amount of alcohol filling it. I feel calmer than earlier, less consumed by my own thoughts; I'm still tired but a content, relaxed kind of tired. The in-between state when inhibitions are down and thoughts become carefree but not yet where they become careless and wayward. A soothing, relaxed state of mind, although not far from the tipping point where regret lives. I sense that line nearing with each mouthful, a line Christian would practically drag me away from if he were here.

Sasha approaches, seeming to read my mind with a bottle in one hand and a dangerous smile across her face. "Look at what Sasha has brought you, Mr. Foy." She sits next to me once more, places the bottle on the table, and points at it. "This will help you forget about Beckie." She laughs. "Literally."

I let out a long breath. "I don't know, Sasha. I have a full day tomorrow. Right now, I'm buzzed and happy. A few more drinks . . . and who knows what will happen?"

"Exactly," she says. "That is where opportunity exists, and that is how life should be lived."

"I don't know—"

"Just one glass." Picking up the bottle, she opens it and begins to pour. "You've already paid for it." She laughs and hands me the glass. "You may as well drink at least one glass before I take the rest."

She holds her stare, gently nudging my shoulder until I cave. Lifting the glass, I hold it to my nose for a second, inhale and consume the aroma, and then drink, filling my throat and letting it linger on my tongue. It feels harsh at first but quickly softens.

"One drink," I say, sipping again from my glass and swilling the whiskey across my gums.

I say the words, but I know they're not true. This won't be my last drink. It should be. I should place the glass on the table, say good-bye to everyone, and head home so I can finally get a solid night's sleep. I should wake up in the morning refreshed, exercise, and write in my journal, just like I used to. I should try meditation again and read and make a healthy breakfast. I should be ready with time to spare before my first call, allowing my mind to clear, so I can own the day and be in control of everything that happens. I should, but I won't. This drink tastes too good, and, as Sasha says, I've already paid for the bottle. The damage is already done.

All that awaits me at home is an empty bed and those nagging thoughts of Beckie that will no doubt keep me awake most of the night. I finish the rest of the glass in one long swallow, sink back into the seat, and welcome the oblivion.

FOUR.

Ferdinand's Bedroom, San Francisco

My eyes shoot open. The first thing I notice is my chest, the feeling that someone is sitting on it. My breath is fast. Out of control. Panting and clinging to the air as it comes in, each one providing nowhere near enough oxygen. The light stings my eyes, and my head . . .

My head!

I let out a groan, my skull's contents seeming to spin and shake simultaneously. The white ceiling is bright. Too bright. I continue to pant and gasp for air, and I feel the sweat form on my forehead, trickling down my cheeks. My throat feels dry as it heaves in air. And my stomach twists and turns and rolls over itself.

Am I awake? Is this still a dream? What is happening?

I try to move but can't. The picture around me becomes clear, the familiar surroundings of my room. I'm in my bed. I'm naked. The sheets around me soaked through, not just my forehead sweaty but my thighs and chest and neck; everything my hands touch is wet and clammy. My breath begins to calm, slightly. Less hectic. Less out of control. Although, I still feel panic. Afraid, even. I'm not sure why. I close my eyes, trying to focus on one thought. I can't as my mind hops from one thing to another, trying to piece together the moment. I try to move again and this time, budge my body and legs ever so slightly. They ache. Everything aches.

I groan again, rolling to my side.

Who is she?

She lays there, still asleep and also naked. Blonde hair covers half her face, her mouth agape and mascara smudged across her cheek.

Who. Is. She?

Groaning again, I roll my entire body over, so I don't have to face this stranger. Snippets of my recent past flood forward: of the club, last night, dancing, and broken glass. An empty bottle—one I'm sure I drank mostly myself. Sasha laughing, introducing me to new people. Wrapping my arms around them, hugging them and smiling, leaning close and kissing them on their cheeks. I shut my eyes tight, not wanting to recall any of it, but all it leads to is the intensified realization of what is happening on the inside of my body, the poison seeming to run through my veins, attacking each limb. My stomach feels empty, as though I've already thrown up. And then, I remember the toilet and my head practically inside of it.

I nudge myself over to the side of the bed and work my legs off, pushing up into an upright position, letting out a weak whimper as I do. Leaning on my knees, I hold my head in my hands, realizing why I woke up in a panic, sweaty and panting and feeling out of control.

"That dream," I say, quietly.

I'm climbing a mountain, wind and rain attacking my face. The icy cold works its way under my jacket, numbing my limbs. I have no gloves on. My fingers and toes . . . they're so cold. I cannot see more than a few feet in front of me, the wind and rain creating a solid wall, like frosted glass. I try to speak, to yell for help, but no words come out. I'm looking for someone. I've lost someone. I'm desperate to find them. I'm scared. I'm scared they are gone forever. I don't know who, but I can feel that they were there. They were next to me, but I lost them. I'm scared. I feel terrified, like a child desperate to find his parents. I edge forward, slowly, running my hands across the jagged rock, my feet barely fitting on the slim ledge that stands between me and the endless drop below. Above me, all I see is a vertical rock face. Below me, nothing but darkness and the swirling wind that seems to form a sea of haunted faces. I feel a dread deep in my stomach, as though the moment has come. I cannot go on. I'm so tired, so cold, so scared and fragile. I begin to cry, tears mixing with the relentless rain. My eyes blur, but there, just in front but out of reach, a darkened figure; a silhouette on the other side of the frosted glass. I wonder if that's who I'm looking for. I try to speak and call out to them. But again, nothing leaves me. *Is it them? It has to be them.* I hear a muffled voice, but I cannot make out the words over the wind. I move my hands across the rock and navigate my feet along the ledge, slowly moving along. Bit by bit. Step by step. I'm close. Almost there. Just another step, but then, below me, the ground breaks, and I lose my footing. I push my fingers into the rock, but that too crumbles. I'm slipping, losing balance, clinging on, but there's nothing to cling on to. I try to scream, but still nothing comes out as the ledge gives way, and I fall into the abyss.

Falling. Falling. Floating.

I wake up each time, gasping for air. It's the third—no, fourth time I've had this exact same dream over the last few months. It's so vivid. It feels so real. I'm there, experiencing the pain and the icy cold. Head still in hands, I slow down my breathing and try to calm my thoughts. "It's just a dream," I say. "Pull yourself together." My heart continues to race, a sense of panic and anxiety refusing to budge. "It's just a dream," I whisper. "Just a stupid dream."

Raising my head, I focus on my surroundings. I'm in my room. I'm safe. It's the same room I wake up in each morning. Light pours in through the floor-to-ceiling window that looks out over green hillsides and beyond to the endless ocean that reaches out to the horizon. A flawless blue sky rests above, and faint streaks of white clouds are all that disturb it. A heap of clothes rests on the floor, made up of mine and the stranger's. I twist my neck to make sure she's still there. Yep, unmoved and unconscious.

As I make a move to finally stand, my phone vibrates on the table to my right. I pick it up and shove it to my ear before it disturbs the person whom I do not wish to face just yet.

"Hello," I say, the word difficult to speak. My throat is desperately dry, like a dessert lost to time.

"Ferdinand?"

"Christian, what time is it?"

"Nearly time for your first call. I thought I better make sure you were up. From the sound of you, it's a good thing I did."

"I feel like I'm going to die."

"Heavy night?"

I burp; it burns my throat. "Yeah. You could say that. I don't remember much of it, and there's some blonde girl lying unconscious in my bed."

"Oh. Not Beckie, I take it?"

"No." I push myself up to my feet and walk toward the window, the bright light soothing my broken body. "You don't know what happened by any chance? I didn't call you or anything?"

"Afraid not. I was asleep by ten. No messages. No voicemail. Nothing out of sorts on your Instagram, either."

"Well, that's good. I suppose."

"It is. So, the girl?"

"I don't know. One of Sasha's friends, maybe. I need to wake her up." I sigh, shaking my head and rubbing my tender eyes. "The calls this morning?"

"They're internal, so don't worry, you don't need to impress. Just stay awake and listen. You should be fine."

"And I need to be out of the house by when?"

"Union Street Recording Studio at twelve. That interview, remember?"

"Oh . . . yeah."

"Look, I'll come over soon with a smoothie and some food. Grab a quick shower, wake up the random girl, and answer your phone when Dave calls. You have twenty minutes. I'll be over as soon as I can."

"Okay. Thanks."

I drop the phone on the floor and lean my head against the glass. Although still early, the sun feels tender on my eyes, cheeks, neck, and shoulders. My insides continue to rumble and spin and spiral out of control. I feel like I could throw up, although I doubt there's anything left inside. I feel empty and dehydrated, my skin paper thin, as though it will tear open if I move suddenly. I need water, but the thought of putting anything into me sets my stomach off. I've been in this situation before. More times than I would like to admit. But this, this is worse than usual. I seem to have not only let loose last night but raged until the end.

Yet as broken as my body and its insides feel, it's the strange sense of fear that consumes me. That dream. That stupid dream. It shakes me each time. I couldn't focus for hours last time around, on edge for most of the morning. The falling. The sense I had lost someone. The helplessness and feeling that I had reached the end. No more energy. No more fight.

"It's just a dream," I say, frustrated that I'm thinking about it all. "It means nothing." I take a deep breath in, hold it there for a second, and try to take in a little more air. My cheeks bulge and my throat tingles, but I remain still and focus on my beating heart. I let out the air all at once and lean my back on the glass, facing the girl on my bed and shaking my head. "Good night, Ferdinand. Good night."

FIVE.

One Union Studios, San Francisco

I stare at a vacant screen. I can't make out the color of my eyes in my reflection, but I sense the blue isn't as piercing as usual. They sting, the skin around them still tight. I feel better than earlier, edging back toward normalcy. My head no longer thuds, and my throat isn't as dry, but my eyes remain heavy and strained, and most of my body aches.

I spent the morning on calls, vaguely listening to issues, ideas, and updates. I attempted to listen and care about what each person said, but my mind kept wandering to last night in its attempt to piece together the puzzle. Snippets kept returning, but they provided nothing of any substance. Christian arrived with food and supplies, and I awoke the strange girl and offered her breakfast. A friend of Sasha's, apparently, named Beth. She added little to the mystery, also drunk and unable to remember much of the night.

I keep thinking about the dream, too, it lingering in my mind longer than usual. The falling. The real, tangible sense of fear. The sodden sheets and panting breaths. I shake the images from my head as soon as they appear. *It's just a dream. It's all fine.*

I sigh and lean back in the leather chair. "Come on," I mutter under my breath. "Where is this guy?"

The studio door opens, and a man heads toward me. I assume it's Jordan.

"Hey, Ferdinand," he says. "Sorry to keep you waiting."

"It's fine." I lean forward to shake his hand. "What's the theme of this interview? Anything I need to know?"

"I do have some questions in mind, but I like to see where the conversation goes," he says. He sits in the chair next to me and picks up a pair of clunky headphones. "Your assistant already sent me some details, so I'll record the intro and outro separately. Right now, we'll dive into the main interview, if that's okay with you."

"Sure."

The studio door flies open again, and a guy with glasses rushes through.

Jordan introduces us: "This is my producer, Jason."

"Hey. Nice to meet you," says Jason. He sits next to the audio mixer and pulls an even larger pair of headphones over his head.

"All right," says Jordan, "I like to keep things informal and relaxed. But I also like to go deep and push for value. So, I'll likely have follow-up questions as we go along. It's all conversational, though."

I nod. "Sure, no problem. I've done this a million times before."

"Cool. Jason has a few tests to run. We'll be ready in a minute. I know we're already a little behind, so we'll kick straight in. That okay with you?"

"Sure. I'm ready."

"Cool. So, how is everything with you, anyway?" he asks. "Must be an exciting time after the recent round of investment."

"Yeah, it's good. The whole business has changed a lot over the last few years. Lots of growth. Lots of new projects and some massive clients. The recent investment capped it all off."

"I bet," he says, looking toward Jason. "Okay, we're just about ready. I think our listeners would love to hear the process you went through to get that investment. You've gone through it a few times, so it will be good to hear what you've learned along the way." He slides his headphones into place. Exchanging a quick look with Jason, he leans back in his chair and pulls the overhead microphone between us. "Ferdinand, welcome to the show."

"Thanks. Happy to be here."

"You recently completed a pretty serious round of investment for Contollo. It must be an exciting time around the office."

"Yeah, it's been an awesome few months," I say, leaning back again and surveying the room. "We have a great team that keeps pushing us to the next level. A lot of my focus recently has been on investment, so we can keep growing and scaling."

"That must be intense for you, being as young as you are. You're, what, twenty-five years old?"

"Just turned twenty-six."

"Right. You must have been working with some big-time investors for this round."

"Yeah," I say, smiling. I look at the screen over Jason's shoulder and watch the audio levels spike up and down. "It's cool. I have some great people on the board who have some serious connections, and I made some myself while at college."

"And this most recent round of investment was for—"

"Eighty-five million," I interrupt. I break into another smile as I think back to the celebrations of a few weeks ago, when we got the all clear after months of late nights and hustling.

"Right. I bet you have some big plans for it. But I guess what I'm really interested in is . . . what does it feel like as a twenty-six-year-old closing that sort of deal? What was your role in it?"

"Well, I am the face of the company. I'm always part of those talks," I say. "I've been doing this for a long time now. I closed a ten million dollar round on my own at the end of my freshman year at Stanford. At that stage, it was just me and a few buddies who helped me with the coding and tech. It was a lot of fun, and I was lucky enough to meet some A-listers at Stanford. One person would buy into the product, love it, tell someone else they knew about it, and it grew from there.

"By the time I finished my second year there, I'd passed all the coding, backend, and tech work to other people. That way, I could focus more on sales and investment. It's crazy, but I remember thinking at the time how ten million dollars was a huge deal. I couldn't imagine going through the whole investment process again. But we did, so I dropped out of Stanford to focus all my energy on the business, and it led to another round of investment, this time for thirty million. And it was huge, you know?"

Jordan nods.

"It was around that stage that I started to make a name for myself, appearing on TV and in magazines and winning awards. It was crazy, and it all seemed to happen overnight. But it was tough, a real hustle-and-grind-kind-of story. Though, I won't lie, I loved it. I've always liked to work hard and challenge myself.

"It's been fun ever since. Massive growth, huge progress compared to the early days: two hundred plus employees, an experienced board of directors who have worked with some of the best companies in Silicon Valley, over a million users, and an 850-million-dollar valuation, which, if I'm honest, doesn't tell the whole story, not with this new round of investment.

"We have big plans, and, between you and me, I think we'll be the next hundred-billion-dollar company that goes public," I add with a wink.

My hangover barely lingers now that the adrenaline ignites my insides with a fresh buzz as each word flows from my mouth.

But Jordan just stares at me. "Okay. Cool." He arches a brow. "Thanks for the overview. But what about *your* role in this investment? Our listeners have businesses of their own, and some of them are growing fast and are desperately in need of investment. You've gone through the process three times: ten million, thirty million, and now eighty-five million. What's the process you went through?"

"Sure, sure," I reply, clearing my throat. "Well, it's all about having the right meetings with the right people and showing them your growth and plans. Like, what have you achieved over the last few years? What does success look like today? What will success look like tomorrow?

"All investors really want to hear about is their return. If they invest now, what will it be worth to them in a few years? Why is your company going to be the next hundred-billion-dollar unicorn? What makes you unique? For us, we've always had a great product that works. From day one, we've created a platform, which modern-day business needs, bringing together their project management and team communication. Whether you have a team of fifty or fifty thousand, our platform helps everyone work at one hundred percent efficiency.

"Our product works. Our marketing is sexy. And, without sounding too into myself, it helps that someone like me is the

CEO. I'm young, and I had huge success while still at Stanford. When I'm in a meeting with an investor, I remind them of Zuckerberg or Dorsey. Combine that with a growing company and a successful product . . . we've had a lot of people who want to invest in us."

I smile, expecting the conversation to move on as it always does during interviews like this.

But Jordan continues to stare, eventually rubbing his chin. "Yeah, but, dude," he finally says, "like, what did you actually do? So far, you're saying you get investment if you have the right connections, you have an already successful business, and you're young. But what do you have to do to get the meeting in the first place? Don't you have to put together some sort of pitch? And how long does all this take? Is it one meeting and, then bang: eighty-five million wired to your account?"

I force a laugh and grit my teeth. *Who is this guy? Why has Christian hooked me up with someone like him? What's he thinking?*

"No, it's not that simple," I say. "It takes time. This last round of investment was three or four months in the making. And I must have had a dozen or more meetings, meals and drinks, and lots of late nights. It's a dance . . . you know how it is."

"Well, no," says Jordan. "I can't say I do. I've had meetings with investors before but not for eighty-five million."

"Right, well, look, whether it's for a million or one-hundred million, the dance is the dance. You've got to be good at talking, and you've got to tell them what they want to hear. If you do that, you're all set."

"So, what did you do during this whole investment round? Was your job just to have meetings and drinks?"

"There was a little more to it than that."

"Like what?"

"Come on, man," I say, looking around the room. "What is this? I didn't know I was coming on here to get grilled. People are usually grateful to have me on their show."

Jordan smiles. "Dude, no offense. I'm a fan of yours, and I personally use Contollo. I'm stoked to talk to you right now, but you being here isn't doing me a favor. All I care about is giving my audience the best value possible. So far, all you've given me is a bunch of elevator pitches."

I shake my head. "You kidding me?" I mutter under my breath.

"Look," he continues. "I value my time, and I value yours. Most of all, I value my audience. We don't do fluff on this show. I want to make this interview work. But we need more than, *know the right people and take them out for drinks.* So, let's rewind this a little. Other than being part of the meetings, what was your actual role during this investment?"

I take a deep breath. "Okay. Well, I reached out to my network, and signed off on the proposals, and—"

"Anything specific you can offer our listeners in terms of real advice they can apply?" he asks.

I stifle a laugh. "If you're in a position to raise investment like this, a lot of that stuff is probably already taken care of."

"By who?"

"Someone on your team."

"But when you raised the first ten million, you did it all yourself, right?"

"Sure. But it still came down to the relationships. That's the main thing."

"How did you get those?"

I pause. "I was at Stanford, bro. You get to know who you need to know."

Jordan sighs and shakes his head. "So, your advice is to get into Stanford?"

"Come on, that's not what I'm—"

"Ferdinand," he begins before turning to Jason. "I think we'll cut it there." He looks back at me. "Dude, I don't want to waste your time on an interview I won't publish. And I'll be honest with you, we won't publish this."

"Are you kidding me? This is a podcast, not *60 Minutes*."

He smiles again. "Maybe not, but this podcast is my work. Everything we publish reflects on me, and that matters. I'm sure you can appreciate that."

I sigh. "Sure, but—"

"At the end of the day," he continues, "all I care about is giving my audience the best information I can. That's what sets us apart. It's why I don't see this as 'just another podcast.' We don't do episodes that are a glorified ad or designed to massage the guest's ego, but so far, you've offered nothing interesting or helpful. No offense, but you've basically said you need to know the right people to get investment and that you need to go to a school like Stanford to meet those people. Imagine listening to that, sitting at home, building your business from nothing . . . do you really think that will help anyone?"

I look at the floor.

"Jason, give us a minute, will you?" Jordan rolls his chair closer, waiting for his colleague to leave before leaning in. "Look, I say it how it is. I have a high standard for this show, and this interview hasn't met it. I'm sorry I've wasted your time, and, honestly, it's on me. We usually stop this from happening during the application process. I guess we dropped the ball with you. I'm sorry about that. It's my fault. But I have to do what's right for the show."

"Okay, fine," I say, curtly. "Whatever."

"We can arrange to do another interview later in the year, if you like."

"Sure. Fine."

"Okay. So, we're cool?"

I place my hands on my thighs and push myself up. "Yeah. It's just not what I was expecting this morning, that's all. I have the hangover for the ages, and I've done a thousand interviews like this before. I wasn't expecting . . . you, I guess."

Jordan smiles as he rises. "What can I say? I say what I need to." He flips through some loose sheets of paper on a nearby desk. "And look, if you do want to do this again in the future, we can. Next time, we'll prepare you properly and make sure you bring your A-game."

I laugh. "You really do say it like it is, don't you?"

"It's the only way. I don't see the point otherwise."

For some reason, I picture the blurred silhouette from my dream. My chest tightens and my stomach rolls, and I begin to feel the same panic from this morning as I awoke mid-fall. "What are you doing now?" I ask.

"Nothing. Now that this interview isn't happening, I have a few hours to kill."

"You want to grab some lunch," I say, although I have no idea why.

SIX.

Kama Sushi, San Francisco

I look at my gyoza: five deep-fried dumplings filled with vegetables. I didn't order them. Jordan did. I haven't had sushi for years. Steam rises from them, creating a haze between the two of us. Jordan picks at his own platter of raw fish, seaweed, and whatever else.

I arrange my chopsticks between my fingers and take in the surroundings. Wooden cladding fills the room, reaching up each wall and across the ceiling. If it weren't for the dark floor, this place would look more like a sauna than a restaurant.

Still, it's supposed to be the best sushi place in San Francisco. Jordan said as much as we climbed into our Uber shortly after leaving his studio. I spent much of the brief trip on the phone, asking Christian to cancel my next few meetings.

I'm not sure why I'm here. I'm even less sure why I invited Jordan to lunch. Going by the look on his face when I asked him, he was surprised, too. A strange compulsion came over me. I asked the question before I even had a chance to question it.

This crazy dream! It has my thinking all over the place.

Still, I've always been curious by people who work from their own rulebook. I'm used to people showing caution around me, nervous when we first meet. But this guy? From the moment we shook hands, he exuded confidence—arrogance. Even now, he focuses more on his food than on me, appears oblivious to the silence between us. I sense that, of the two of us, I'm the more uncomfortable.

"So," I pipe up, "your podcast. How long have you been doing it?"

He wipes his mouth and clears his throat. "Almost ten years. Although this current version is new. I used to host another show but left to start my own. The format is pretty much the same, though."

"That's a long time for a podcast. I take it you've interviewed a lot of people in that time."

He nods. "So, let's get to it, man. Why are we here?"

I laugh slightly. "I'm wondering that myself. I guess I'm curious. I don't meet many people who say it 'like it is,' like you do."

Jordan smirks. "I'm impatient, and I have a low tolerance for bull. I don't see the point in hiding from what I have to say."

"How does that work out for you?" I ask.

"Honestly? Fine. It upsets some, but most of the people I care about appreciate it or, at least, respect it. I hate wasting time."

"I can respect that. There's never enough of it to waste."

He places his chopsticks on the table and leans toward me. "Look, I apologize for having to cancel the interview. It's on me and my producer. We should have got it on point long before you came on. You had a wasted journey, and for that, I'm sorry. But

I won't apologize for making the decision I did. As I said at the studio, I value my audience above all else. So, if that's why we're here—"

"It's not. I'm not entirely sure why we are here, but we're cool."

He nods, biting into a fresh piece of sushi. "Okay, good." He takes a deep breath and looks through the glass door at the busy streets of San Francisco. "I was just expecting more from you, that's all. I like to go deep. What you were offering . . . it's just surface-level fluff that helps nobody."

"You're not one to build up someone's confidence, are you?"

"You need it?" he asks, smiling. "From the sound of it, you have plenty of people around you who say yes."

"What does that mean?" I say. "I don't surround myself with 'yes men.'"

"No?"

"No. I have people who challenge me. I'm the youngest on the board by a long shot. And we have a great team; they never tell me what I want to hear. I've seen as much rejection as anyone."

"Yeah?" He probes, an incredulous look across his face.

I lean forward a little. "You think I built an 850-million-dollar company on handouts? I've had to hustle and grind the entire way."

"So you said." He picks up his chopsticks and grabs another piece of sushi. "Look, I don't want to offend you, so, if you want to have a meal and chat about whatever, that's cool with me. But if you want to get real, well, I have a few questions I'd love to ask you."

"Like what?"

"Are you sure you want to hear them?"

I nod though I'm not.

"What is it that you actually do?" he asks.

I say nothing, my fingers pressing into my legs.

"I mean, no offense," he says again, "because I know you're busy, and you're a CEO, and let's face it, you outdo me in pretty much every department. But I've followed you for years. Between what I've read recently and our interview, I'm finding it hard to figure out what your role is these days."

I puff out my cheeks and lean back in my chair. "And I'm not supposed to take offense at that?"

"That's up to you, isn't it? This is what I do: I ask questions. I have no control over how people answer or whether they like the questions I ask."

"What if I asked you that?" I counter. "Would you take offence?"

"Not at all. I can tell you what my role is, and I can tell you what I do each day."

I shake my head. "Okay, fine, I'll play ball. I'm the CEO. I have other people around me doing the work and running the business. I oversee everything, have meetings, and focus on new partnerships and strategies."

"Like the new round of investment?"

"Exactly."

"But what did you do during all that?"

"I told you earlier," I say. "I had meetings. I told the investors about the future and what we have planned. If it wasn't for me, we wouldn't have got that eighty-five million. I'm the face of the whole company. You think Elon Musk or Jeff Bezos or Mark Zuckerberg spend all day at a desk? No! They're in one meeting after another. That's all they do. Maybe you don't get that because you don't own a company as big as mine."

My heart is racing, my fists clenched. I look at Jordan; he seems unfazed. He places another piece of sushi in his mouth and appears to consider his words. "So, what's the plan?"

"For what?"

"For Contollo. You say you told the investors about the future and what you have planned. What is it?"

The script is still fresh in my mind after months of rehearsing and rehashing it. "We're working on the next version of the software, which will open us up to almost any industry on the planet. Once we—"

"No, no," he says, interrupting me. "What I mean is, what do you have planned for the business? *You!* It's your company, right? You built it from nothing. Surely you have a plan for it—a dream, a vision. A purpose that drives you to do what you do?"

"Well, it's to go public and for me to become a billionaire."

"Okay. Then what?"

"What do you mean?"

"Why do you want to be a billionaire?" he asks, a chopstick in each hand.

"Who wouldn't want to be? Once you become a billionaire, you reach a level of success few others ever achieve. It's a club I've always dreamed of joining."

"Really? Always?"

"Yes."

"Why? What would you be able to get with a billion dollars that you can't with the millions you already have?"

I laugh. "A lot of things. But it's not about the money."

"So, what is it?"

"Power, for one. And respect. If I'm being honest, it's not about the money at all. I like money, but it's not everything."

"So, why is becoming a billionaire your purpose?"

"It isn't. But when you reach a level that makes money irrelevant, to an extent, you reach a level where anything is possible."

He continues to push. "Like what?"

"I don't know . . . freedom, for one. True freedom."

"Freedom?"

"Yeah, freedom. With a billion dollars, you experience freedom like nothing else."

"Really? Like what?"

"Everything. You're free from everything: restraint, responsibility. When you experience true freedom like that, you can be happy. Truly happy. The impossible becomes possible. Nothing is out of reach."

"True happiness," he says, nodding his head. "What does that look like to you?"

"Everything I've just said."

He laughs. "That's the problem, Ferdinand. You didn't say much of anything. You basically said that you have a dream of becoming a billionaire so you can join an exclusive club where freedom and happiness exist, but that money isn't actually what matters to you." He shakes his head. "Maybe I'm missing something, but that doesn't make much sense. And, honestly, I don't buy it. Becoming a billionaire doesn't make you free or happy. It certainly doesn't give you anything you couldn't have with a few million to your name."

"Have you ever spoken to a billionaire?" I snap.

"Yeah. A few of them. Have you?"

"Of course I have."

"And that's what you learned from them? That money makes you happy. That the bigger you become, the easier it gets? That the only way to have freedom is to make a few billion?"

"Well, no—"

"Then what? What happens when you make a billion? Do you then have to make two . . . or three . . . or ten? Do you need to become the richest? Where does it end?"

"No. Like I say, it's not about the money."

"What is it about? You have this company you created in college, and it's great. It's an awesome tool, bro. I use it. I love it. And if your purpose is to make life easier for people like me, and if the reason you want to make a billion is so you can serve more people, that's cool. If that's the dream, fine.

"But that's not what I'm hearing. All I hear is talk about some exclusive club that, once you join, life suddenly makes sense. Look, I'm still trying to figure life out like everyone else, but I know enough to know that no 'club' or amount of money fixes your problems. If you're unhappy now, more money won't make you less unhappy."

"Who says I'm unhappy?" I say sharply, annoyed at the suggestion. "I am happy. I have a great life. I have a great company, one I started from nothing."

"From nothing?"

"Yeah, from nothing. I didn't have a trust fund. I got into Stanford on my own merit, earning a scholarship. I'm not one of those rich frat boys who's given everything in life. I had no help."

"Really?"

I grit my teeth. "Yeah, really."

"Calm down, dude," he says, holding up both hands. "I'm just asking questions." He leans in, pushing his plate to one side. "Look, as I said earlier, I've followed you for years. You built Contollo on your own, and you deserve to have what you have today. I'm in awe of what you've achieved, which is why your apparent lack of vision annoys me. "

I stare at him, aghast. *Who is this guy? Who does he think he is, speaking to me like this?*

"But come on. You did not start with nothing. You were at Stanford, dude. You had access to the right people, people with money to turn your good idea into a reality. My guess is your first few clients were Stanford alumni, right?"

I grit my teeth and look away from him.

"Yeah, I thought so. And that doesn't take anything away from what you've achieved. You're a talent. You had a great idea, and you had the hustle to get it done. But you had access to the people, money, and opportunity that ninety-percent of people do not have."

"Okay, sure," I say. "But I earned my way into Stanford."

"Yeah, you did. You're as smart as anyone, and I imagine school was easy for you. Right?"

I feel anger bubble and build; my fingers bundled tight into my palms beneath the table.

"Again, I'm not saying you didn't work hard to get there, but you went to a private school. Your father's a professor and your mother's a publicist. Between them, they'll have a huge network. They might not have funded your business, but I'm guessing they gave you a darn good upbringing." He smiles and leans in again. "Let me guess, you had a tutor growing up?"

"Yeah, so what?"

"A few of them, right?"

I shrug.

"What about summer camp and other stuff outside of school?"

"Sure."

"And your parents helped you with homework?"

"Yeah, of course," I say. My tone is quick, harsh.

"And they were supportive? And they loved you? They gave you their time and attention?"

I shrug again.

"This is the problem," he says. "People like you and me trick ourselves into thinking we're self-made and that we started from scratch. You kidding me? You're not self-made. There are people out there who grew up with no parental support, who went to some awful school with teachers who didn't give a crap about them, in a neighborhood that typically sets them up for a life in crime.

"They have to fight for everything, and if they do manage to make it to college and graduate, they face a society that forces them to jump through hoops based on the color of their skin or the country they're from. What hoops have you had to jump through?"

I look at my 800-dollar shoes that I don't even like. My anger seems to dissipate; my insides feel heavy.

"Your parents may not have funded your start-up," Jordan continues gently, "but my guess is they would have supported you had you failed. There wasn't much risk for you, but there was a whole lot of reward. Some people know if they fail, that's it: debt, bankruptcy, putting their family in danger, they're out on the streets. That's real risk, dude. Are you telling me you would have faced all that had Contollo failed?"

"No," I say.

He scratches his chin. "None of this makes you a bad person. I had the same opportunities and privilege as you. And, although I know I have a better work ethic than most, it doesn't take away from the fact that I was set up to succeed. Not everyone has that, which is why it's important you do what you do for the right reasons."

"So, what? I'm not doing what I'm doing for the right reasons? I should shut it all down to go build houses in Peru?"

He laughs, picking up his drink. "No. People who preach that stuff drive me crazy."

"So, what? What's your point?"

"My point," he says, clearing his throat, "is that you get one shot at this. You have everything you need to change the world and make it a better place. What it is you'll do, I have no idea. But you're smart and young; you have talent and charisma and access to all the money and connections you need. I have no doubt you could join the billionaires' club, but unless there's a reason for it, what's the point? Will you really be happy? Will you look back on your life as an old, withered man and say, 'Yeah, I made the best of it'?

"All I know is, I've met a lot of people over the last ten years. Some have been at the beginning of their journeys, and some are way down the line. I've hung out with people who have no money and those with a few billion to their name. I have friends with big businesses and friends with really small businesses. And, in general, none of that determines whether they're happy.

"Some of them are. Some of them aren't. Some are seen as successful people and placed on some crazy pedestal by society. But it doesn't mean they feel successful on the inside. But I know some people who make fifty grand a year who are happy, successful, free, and all the other stuff we desire to feel.

"They know what they want. They have a dream and a vision. They have something that gives them a reason to do what they do. *Those* people are the happy ones. It's when I realized this that I personally let go of all the other nonsense that held me back. Which was a lot, by the way, because I also used to focus on money and fame and trying to prove everything to people who don't matter.

"You want to know how and why I speak my mind like I do? Because I don't care what people think anymore. I know who I am. I know what I'm doing. I know I don't have it all figured out, but I do know what success is and isn't to me. Do you? Have you ever even questioned it?"

The buzz of the restaurant takes over, silence falling between the two of us once more.

I look at him. I have no idea what to say. My chest feels empty. I want to counter and prove him wrong, list reasons why I do what I do, and break down my dreams, vision, and purpose for the future.

But I can't. "Geeze," I say under my breath. I rub my hands across my face. "I guess I used to. But lately . . ."

"You know what's really sad about that?" he replies, picking up his drink once more. "That's true for most people. They follow a path they think they want, rather than taking the time to figure out what they actually do want."

I lean back in my chair, staring at the space above Jordan's head. Lights dangle from the ceiling in a row, casting shadows above. He continues to talk. I watch as he makes animated gestures, though my mind is lost, caught in an internal loop of questions I used to ask myself that have lain dormant for a long time. My heart races once more, just like it did this morning. That panic returns, a tight chest with it. I remember how I felt when I woke up and how I did watching Beckie leave the restaurant. I figured I had it all figured out, but now, with chopsticks below me and food that's growing cold, I'm unsure of what I know; I'm doubting the truths I believe to be true.

SEVEN.

Ferdinand's House, San Francisco

I stare at the TV as faces flash up and vanish, one channel flicking to the next before I'm able to decide what show is what. I stare, taking in nothing but the blurred colors, my thumb numb from pressing the same button for so long. I don't like TV. Never have, not even as a kid. I preferred to read or lose myself in a computer screen rather than waste away in front of stories and conversations that held little significance in my life.

Despite this, I have a TV. A huge one.

I recall the person who delivered it, maybe five months ago. A top of the range set, apparently. It has all the latest features a TV fanatic could ask for. I can't remember what it cost—three, four thousand dollars? Maybe more.

I haven't sat here and watched it more than three or four times. This house is full of empty and meaningless desires like it. Only, am I the one who desires them? This couch is too white and leathery for my liking. Yet I not only bought it but paid more than ten grand for it. Then there's the coffee table my feet rest on—a huge chunk of wood that cost more than my parents' first family car, the same car that drove me to school and football practice, to this place and that.

There's more technology in this house than I imagine many schools have access to. I can speak a demand in any room and have lights turned up, temperature turned down, and the oven switched on while I have drinks across town.

Not that I've ever used the oven.

I have it all: the latest specs, the hottest trends, and the most sophisticated solutions. And yet, I use so little of it, so little of the time. It all just exists, and after this afternoon, I'm beginning to wonder if maybe I do, too. Just exist.

I halt the flickering screen and turn it to black, tossing the remote out of reach. I sigh, observing the room as the air slowly departs my lungs. A wall of glass separating me from the dark outside world of San Fran. A palm tree springing up out of the shiny grey floor, hanging over the stairs that lead up to a colorful bookcase full of books I have not read. A flawless, sparkling clean kitchen to my left that I don't recall ever cooking in. And, all around me, obscenely patterned cushions I did not choose and do not like.

I own this house and everything in it. But is it my home?

When I think of home, I picture my parents and the house I grew up in. But I haven't lived there for almost a decade. I have lived here for four years yet spend so little time within these walls. I don't stay in and watch TV or read, and I never sit on this couch and enjoy the view. I post pictures of this impressive place and share it with the world, and I invite people to stay with me and enjoy the unnecessary comforts. Then we spend all our time out and about, enjoying further unnecessary comforts, which a city like San Francisco offers.

I never do this—sit here, doing nothing. I never just *think* for the sake of thinking, for the chance to explore what's actually on my mind.

Yesterday, I woke up satisfied and confident about the journey ahead. I awoke an entrepreneur with purpose, a CEO with a vision, and a man with the wealth, talent, and ambition to achieve everything. Some thirty hours later, as the dark closes in for another night, a heavy, sad, and numbing rumble consumes me. Jordan, in less than an hour, broke me. Beckie left me. I don't feel like me.

I pick up my phone and bring it to life, the home screen once again notifying me of all the messages, calls, and notifications I've missed. I'm wanted, in demand, and needed by so many. Yet I've spent all evening wondering if this is true, or if it's my own feeling of self-importance.

I want it to be true. I want to believe it is. I am sure it is. Only . . .

A vibration interrupts my thought and Christian's name appears on the screen.

"Hey," I say.

"You're alive," he replies, the hum of music in the background. "Is everything okay?"

"Yeah, I'm fine."

"Really?"

"Did you cancel my meetings?"

"I did."

"Any issues? What did you say?"

"Well," he says, laughing, "you didn't give me much to go on and wouldn't answer your phone, so I told them you weren't feeling well."

"Everyone was okay with that?"

"For the most part. What happened?"

"Good," I say as I glance around the living room once more. "What do you think of my house?"

"What do you mean?"

"Do you like it?"

"Sure. It's incredible," he replies.

"What about all the stuff inside it? All the furniture and artwork and . . . stuff?"

"Yeah, it's all great. Why?"

"So you like it?" I press.

"Sure."

"You would like to live in a house like this, then? You like the style and everything, right?"

He clears his throat. "Well, it's not personally my style. It's all a bit much for me. But it suits you."

"It suits me?"

"Sure."

"What does that mean? Why does it suit me and not you?"

"What's all this about, Ferdinand?" he asks. "What happened this afternoon?"

I sigh. "Nothing. I had an interesting conversation earlier. It's left me thinking."

"Thinking about what?"

"Everything, I guess," I say, sighing once more. "About what I'm doing. About what we're doing as a business. About this house and all this stuff and the life I've led the last few years." I take a deep breath and close my eyes. "About the vision. The purpose. The mission. We have one of those, right?"

"You mean on the website?"

"Yeah. What is it?"

"I can send it to you if you'd like."

"You don't know what it is?"

"Do you?" he asks.

"Nope. I'm guessing I came up with it or was in the meeting, but no . . . I have no idea. And neither do you."

"Well," he says, hesitating, "it's to help teams communicate better with one another. And reduce the amount of tools they use. I don't know the exact script, but it's along those lines."

I push up from the couch and walk toward the sliding doors that lead out to the pool. The bright room behind me reflects against the dark backdrop. My reflection stares back. "You've been part of this from almost the beginning," I say, sliding the door to my right and stepping out into the night. "We used to know this stuff. I remember a time when it was the most important thing. We were obsessed with solving a real problem: redefining how communication works. These days, it feels like a script we've created just for investors."

"Ferdinand, are you okay?" Christian asks gently. "I can come over, if you want."

The pool in front glistens, a wrinkled moon spreading across its surface. "I'm fine," I say, staring out toward the horizon. "Just thinking about things is all."

"That's what I'm worried about. It's when you think that my life usually gets harder," he says, a hint of mirth in his words.

I smile. "I'll talk to you in the morning."

As I slide the phone back into my pocket, I hesitate. I bring it back to life and swipe through icons. A few flicks and taps, and I'm where I need to be, holding the phone to my ear and awaiting the sound of a voice.

"Hello," says that voice, interrupting the fifth ring.

"Jordan?"

"Who's this?"

"It's Ferdinand."

"Oh, hey. What's up?"

"What's up?" I say. "This morning I woke up hungover but normal. And then I met you, and now I'm here in my big house full of things I think I might hate and unsure whether I am happy, whether I actually do enjoy my business and my life."

He laughs. "Glad I could help."

"I'm serious," I say, sitting on a lounger a few feet from my pool. "I feel numb. I've done nothing all day but think about the future and where I've come from and how I feel about . . . everything." I hesitate because I'm unsure what I feel and what I should say and why I've called the guy who turned my world upside down.

"I'm sitting here by my pool, and it looks awesome. I love this pool. I've loved this pool since the moment I first came to see this house. But do you know the last time I swam in this pool?"

"I have no idea," he says.

"Neither do I. I can't remember the last time I came outside like this and just looked at the view. I love this view. It's why I bought the house."

My mind wanders, picking out the memory of when I first arrived.

It was a hot summer day. I walked onto the deck, having toured the rest of the house. Each room had stood out, impressive and clean, the poster-boy setup for a tech CEO like me. But it had felt like a house no different from any other. That changed as soon as I stood by the pool, overlooking the bay and the lush, green hillsides separating me from it. A tingle rose in my chest as time seemed to stop. I imagined lounging by the pool while reading or eating dinner with friends as days blended into nights. I needed this place. I put in an offer there and then.

"I don't know where the last few years have gone," I say. "We had a vision. We used to talk about that kind of stuff. I used to wake up early, excited to get into the office and make a difference. And I wanted to make a difference, you know? I didn't want to build a product or make more money or grow for the sake of growing. I wanted to help people. I wanted to do something that would mean something, and . . ." I trail off, staring into the flickering ripples of the pool.

"You don't think you're doing that anymore?" he asks.

"I'm not sure," I say. "This morning, I figured I was. But now? I'm not so sure."

Silence falls over us for a few seconds, the thrum of insects taking over once more.

"When did this change?" Jordan asks.

"I don't know." I sigh. "The entire business just keeps growing. I'm not even aware of half of it. I turn up and get introduced to another new team member. I get ideas and numbers thrown at me. People want me to make a decision, so I end up saying yes.

"And it's working, I suppose. At each board meeting, they talk about how all the right numbers are going up; how the plan is *this*, and it's all going great. All I do is sit there and nod. Act as though I'm in charge. But, in reality—"

"You don't feel like you are?"

"No." I sigh again, this one heavier. "I'm not sure if it's even my business anymore."

"Look, Ferdinand," he says. "I can't really talk right now. I have plans with my wife. But, if I'm honest, I'm not surprised to hear any of this. It's the feeling I got over lunch. You built something amazing. You did that on your terms. These days, it's this massive machine. Maybe, deep down, you never wanted that. Maybe you did. I don't know. It's not like you'd be the first CEO to lose sight of the big picture like that. It happens when you let it; life spirals out of control. All you can do is hope that you wake up before it's too late."

"That's what it feels like right now," I say. "I've been asleep, dreaming. And now, all of a sudden, I'm awake, and the room is spinning."

"It happens, dude."

"Did it happen for you?"

"What? Letting life spiral out of control?"

"Yeah."

"To an extent, sure. Everyone does."

"What did you do?"

"That's a loaded question, man. I did a lot, and there's no simple answer. But I guess I started to ask the right questions. I started to question what I thought I wanted and became suspicious of all the nonsense everyone threw at me. I slowed things down. That's all you can do. You get in this mess because you let yourself go through the motions. You need to get back in control and remember why you started everything in the first place."

"I had that," I say, my heart racing. "I swear, I had such a big vision. I wanted to change the world. I was a force, you know? Always full of energy and excited about the next step. I keep trying to close my eyes and focus on what that used to be like. Each time I do, my head spins. All these thoughts hit me at once." I pinch the corner of each eye between my thumb and finger. "I can't settle on anything. It's like I've woken up from a dream, in a panic." I pause, thinking about the nightmare I woke up from this morning.

There's a crackle of white noise and the distant hush of his breath. "Okay, look," he says, quietly. "I really can't talk right now, but I do hear you. And I feel you, man. I know what it's like to build something and then realize one day you no longer align with it. It's one of the reasons I started my new show. A lot of what you said reminds me of something a friend of mine once told me. Different from you because he came from Wall Street. But one day, he woke up like that." He snaps his fingers. "Began to question it all."

I close my eyes again, my heart racing. *What the heck is going on today?*

"His name is AJ Leon. You know him?"

"No."

"I can hook the two of you up, if you like. I think he might be someone you should speak to."

I take a deep breath, trying to calm the chaos inside my chest. "Sure. Thanks. And sorry. I don't even know why I called. I just—"

"It's all good. I'll send you both a message before I leave for dinner."

"Thanks." I keep the air in my lungs and look up to the night sky.

I lower the phone away from my ear and place it on the pool deck below. I look at it, the background image of me raising a glass of whiskey on a private jet. I recall posting that on Instagram and the continuous checks afterward to see how many comments I received. I didn't reply to a single one but took pride in each ping.

I just stare. Stare at the picture until it fades to black, heavy-chested, sinking further within myself.

EIGHT.

In an Uber, San Francisco

A crowd of people pass beside me as I sit alone in the back of this car, stuck in traffic as I so often am.

In college, I walked everywhere. I owned a car and used it to drive back to see my parents but rarely more than that. I liked to walk and think and imagine. Listening to music, I'd wander through campus and then further drift into the city, amongst the hustle and bustle of people rushing here and there.

I took pleasure knowing I wasn't part of it. I didn't have a nine-to-five to lose myself in. I controlled my life and my freedom, and knew I always would, because I would never, not for a day, work for someone else. I don't know when that changed. I can't remember the moment when my love for walking stopped, replaced by rushing from one Uber to the next.

Today, I walk from cars to office buildings. I walk into my house and out again. I walk to elevators that whisk me up to meeting rooms. I'm fast, intense, and quick to move from this to that.

Where one commitment ends, another has already begun. There's little time to stop. There's never time to step back.

People like me don't have the time to walk. Every moment counts. Each minute is a minute to use wisely. Time spent walking is time spent not in a meeting. If I drive, I cannot check email or tick another task off my to-do list. If I take the time to eat my lunch outside, that's one less meeting, one less talk, or one less conversation with a potentially life-altering individual.

Yet here I am, stuck in a car as life passes me by. I suppose traffic is always like this, but I don't notice it because my head's usually immersed in my phone. Not today. Today, it remains in my pocket as I look out to the world around me and allow my mind to wander. I see the people and the streets and the other cars stuck in this traffic, all busy doing their own thing and lost in their own importance.

They are busy.

They have so much to do.

They are important.

They are everything.

They notice nothing.

I'm one of them. I didn't use to be, and I don't want to be, but I am. I'm worse than most, as days bleed into the evening and then into the night. A quick sleep followed by an abrupt wake-up, I'm tired and groggy, and another day awaits with so many tasks and so little thinking.

I continue to stare out my window as the driver in front taps his steering wheel and hums along to some music. I used to love music. I used to listen to it every single day. New music and old, one genre after another. I listened as I worked, and then I would listen as I walked. I imagine the guy walking past my window with a spring in his step is listening to music. He's young, possibly still in college, with a blue backpack hanging from his shoulder; a giant smile spreads from cheek to cheek. He walks at a clip, dodging men and women who walk toward him, but he doesn't seem to rush like most of the others surrounding him.

I picture myself as he passes the car and then jets off into the crowd.

I used to be him. Before the expensive clothes and the endless Uber rides and the worry that each minute is far too important to waste on such things. I was he, lost in my own little world of endless possibilities. So many of my ideas came about that way. They would start as hazy images, a hint of what might be. The details wouldn't come until later, but the initial inception almost always came in an instant, not as I sat at a desk or jumped on a call, but as I walked and observed the world around me.

I close my eyes and picture a time that seems long ago.

Wandering in Mission Bay, I passed through parks, up and down streets, and by the water for no reason at all. It was during the early days of Contollo, when we were a shell of who we are and what we offer today. We had potential, and we gave our customers a service none of our competitors did. Yet I felt frustrated by where we were. Not because we weren't bigger or worth more, but because we weren't having the impact I knew we could. We were helping people but not solving a problem that was hurting them. For weeks, my mood had been growing grimmer. I couldn't hone in on what our big promise should be. It felt close but not close enough.

"That's it," I said quietly. An idea seemed to spring forward as I looked out toward the bay. A haze of an idea. An incomplete idea. But one that tickled my insides as I rooted through my backpack for a notebook and pencil. Within seconds, I was consumed by the idea, scribbling down words and messy drawings. I couldn't stop. One thought led to the next. The haze gained clarity with each new flick of my wrist.

I wasn't conscious of what happened around me. Time seemed to cease, no longer important or applicable to me. Ten minutes, an hour. I had no idea how much time had passed me by. When I did stop, I dropped the notebook to the ground and stretched out my arms. I ached all over, across my shoulders and down my spine, legs and feet nearly numb from sitting cross-legged for so long.

The sky dimmed. I flipped through my notes, surprised by how many I had made. Dozens of pages that may or may not have made any sense. I smiled, arched my head back and looked to the sky, taking note of the surge of energy roaming within me. I didn't know what impact that idea would have on the business or me. I wasn't sure if it would make as much sense the next day or when I shared it with other people. Yet I recall feeling peaceful, as though I had discovered an answer to a question I had pondered for weeks.

The problem, overcome.

The pain dissolved.

In the days that followed, I explored this inception of an idea, refined and reworked it into something practical. Until that point, conversations with investors had fizzled out quickly. They liked what we were building, but they didn't fall in love with what we could become. This single spark of an idea is what ignited interest and intrigue, transformed like into love, resulting in our first ten-million-dollar investment.

The mere memory of this time fills me with energy, a sliver of the intense adrenaline I felt back then. Not all days were as exciting as that one, but most offered an energy that seems to be missing today. Back then, I thought only about the impact we had. Not the money. Not the market share. Those were by-products of a greater obsession, and only now do I realize that obsession is no more.

The car comes to another halt—another set of lights, another rush of people passing by my window. I feel empty, as though someone has taken every ounce of air out of my lungs. I hold my chest, the touch almost numb. I look around at my surroundings.

Where am I? What am I doing? Where in the world am I going?

I'm on my way to meet a man I have never met and have little knowledge about. Ray arranged this meeting. I'm here doing as I'm told, no questions asked. I'm the head of my company with no clue about what we're doing. *Is this meeting important? Is anything we do as a business important anymore?*

I sink into my seat and hunch my shoulders, pull out my phone and navigate to the message Jordan sent last night, introducing me to AJ. I replied at the time, thanking Jordan and greeting AJ. A few exchanges have occurred since but nothing noteworthy.

He's currently in Stratford-upon-Avon, in the UK, and will remain there for the next week. He recently returned from Africa, having done some sort of philanthropic project I don't quite understand. He used to work on Wall Street but quit his executive job so he could start his own business.

I know almost nothing about AJ, but I keep thinking about how Jordan said, "I think he might be someone you should speak to." He was the first person to come to Jordan's mind. Why? Out of all the people he's interviewed over the years, why him?

I shake my head and sigh. "What am I doing?" I ask under my breath.

I close my eyes and picture the guy I used to be. The dreams he had. The passion he instilled in his everyday life. The vision he created. Would he go to a meeting with this person today?

I open my eyes and take a deep breath. "Hey," I say, leaning forward and placing my hand on the driver's seat. "Change of plan. Can you take me somewhere else?"

"We're only a few minutes away," the driver says, his deep voice drowning out the music.

"It doesn't matter. Can you take me to the airport?"

He twists in his seat.

"There's a good tip in it for you."

He laughs. "Sure thing, boss."

I lean back, gaze out the window, and catch my reflection staring back.

NINE.

Box Brownie, Stratford-Upon-Avon

I stare out the window, bright sunlight shining through. A silhouetted man stands in front of me, blocking much of the view.

People pass by, and the streets are full of those on their lunch breaks and tourists aimlessly looking up at buildings and sights. I did my wandering earlier, taking to the streets of Stratford and visiting churches and birthplaces that link the people of today with Shakespeare's past. I haven't read anything of his since school and didn't particularly enjoy it then. But wandering through the streets he once walked, in a town with so much history and heritage—more so than my entire country can lay claim to—filled me with a kind of hope, peace.

I'd headed straight for the airport, where I rang AJ. He didn't answer, so I stood at the check-in desk, trying to decide what I was actually doing. I planned to jump on the first flight to England, but why? *Why would AJ want to meet me? What did I expect to find? How was I supposed to justify jumping on a plane to go visit a stranger?*

I rubbed my eyes and shook my head, but then my phone rang. It was AJ. His voice sounded kind and calm, as though we had spoken to one another many times before. As soon as I heard his voice, I relaxed and told him nonchalantly that I was at the airport and wanted to see him.

He replied with even more nonchalance: "Sure. I'm busy tomorrow but can meet you the day after."

So I booked a ticket, waited at the airport for five hours, caught the first flight I could, and was soon in London. I can't recall the last time I did anything with such spontaneity, let alone a time I caught a flight without some sort of business meeting awaiting me. I still have no idea what I expect or why I'm here. But I've spent the better part of forty-eight hours alone, most in a country where I know few people. Just me and my thoughts, walking for the sake of walking because I can, and because I haven't in so long.

I sit at a small, white table, one barely big enough to hold two plates. I lean on the black wall to my left, littered with chalk drawings of coffee cups, flowers, and random doodles. It's dark in here, the bright sunshine only reaching a few feet into the room.

I googled AJ while at the airport, realizing I was about to travel across an ocean to meet a guy I knew nothing about. I found his manifesto: *The Life & Times of a Remarkable Misfit.* I downloaded it and read it on the plane. I planned to skim it, but his words captured me and pulled me in.

> *There are times when we sail so far off course, when our dreams are so far from reach that they appear but balmy glimmers, violently strewn on a distant horizon that we will never pierce. When complacency and*

> *compliance, safety and security, have so entranced us that gradual reform is no longer possible. In these moments, we have but one option—revolt.*

That's how his first essay began. My heart sank reading this, and it continued on a rollercoaster ride as I read the rest, at times inspired and dream-like, and at other points, sad and desperate. Images of my dream kept coming forward, the glass-like wall and the feeling of utter hopelessness. Beckie's face, too, and the realization that she's gone. She's no longer just there.

Another sentence sticks in my mind from his first essay: *If you feel like you don't belong where you are right now, maybe you weren't meant to just win. Maybe you were meant to change the world.*

I've spent my life "winning," but I'm not sure how much of it I've spent leaving my mark. I have, on occasion, gotten close with this idea or that, but then I'm pulled off course by the seduction of winning. The problem is, I don't feel happy when I win. As a child, I always felt happiest when I explored and dove down whatever rabbit hole captured my attention: coding, literature, football . . .

Yet the need to *win* always seemed to seduce me.

My love of literature waned as I realized I would never write books as good as those I read. Coding became a job and a business, the beginnings of Contollo, and the empire that's taken over since. Before that was football. The only sport I have ever loved.

Between the ages of ten and fourteen, it's all I talked about. I lived to watch it, read about it, and practice it. As long as I had a football in hand, I felt happy, a sense of peace. I didn't care about being the best—not at first. But the more I practiced, the better I became. I went from running back to quarterback: the leader, the center of the entire team. The best.

I needed to win. I needed to get better. I worked harder and harder, pushing myself further. Then, my love faded to a point where I hated holding a ball. I was no longer the best player on the team. A new quarterback came along, younger and better than me. He took my place. I didn't fight to regain it. I didn't want to. I quit. I fell out of love with the sport. At least, that's what I told myself. I replaced it with a computer screen, coding and hacking my way back to a place that made me happy, a place where time seemed to cease.

I haven't thought about football for years. But on the plane, as I read AJ's twenty-three short essays, I couldn't help it. Did I quit because I fell out of love with it? Or was it because I felt like a failure, no longer good enough? I had stopped winning. Winning was all I had wanted.

Yet it was winning that sapped me of what I loved about the game.

Winning has never made me happy, but it's the only thing I've ever strived for.

A guy walks through the door, removing his sunglasses and looking around the room. He's tall with tanned skin, jet-black hair tied up in a bun, and a thick beard hiding much of his features. He spots me and smiles, striding toward the table as I stand to greet him.

"I'm a hugger," he says, wrapping his arms around me. "It's nice to meet you, Ferdinand."

I flinch, my muscles tensing around my neck and shoulders, my arms hovering inches from AJ's back, unsure what to do. "Oh, hey," I say, stepping away. "Nice to meet you, too. And thank you for this. I know it's—"

"Hold that thought," he says, surveying the room. "Let me grab a drink and say hello to that guy," he continues, pointing to the barista walking in from the back.

The two hug and exchange words as I sit down and drain my coffee cup.

"I love this place," AJ says, joining me. "I was one of their first customers, and this is where a lot of my early work began."

He continues to catch me up on his day, and how he's on the board of The Shakespeare Trust. He and his wife, Melissa, travel the world, working on more projects than I can fathom but often return to Stratford, their spiritual home and inspirational mecca.

"I was always happiest when working in theatre," he said. "But it was Shakespeare. He's all that's ever interested me."

I reply with my own tales and journey and how I've felt in recent days. I speak about the flight, losing myself in his essays—about how they'd captured me.

The son of two Cuban immigrants, he grew up without much and often not enough. But he worked and aspired, desperate to escape the shackles that held his family back, prove everybody wrong, and show the world he wasn't a failure. He turned to finance, Wall Street, and climbed the ladder with charisma and ambition. He climbed, climbed, climbed, one promotion leading to the next, making more money each time but always spending more than what he had.

Until one day, he sat in his corner office and was offered a promotion and sum of money that would clear his debt and keep him clear of it, forever. The sort of money that means you always have enough and the sort of promotion you don't turn down.

"I had this vision of myself as a seventy-year-old man," he said. "He looked back at me, in that office, mourning the life of what could have been. I could not sign that paper," he continued. "Everyone has a price, and the number on that paper was mine."

Despite the fear and the unknown, AJ walked away, not only from that promotion but the life he had led for a decade: the six-figure salary, the huge bonuses, the corner office. All gone mere weeks before he married Mel. The two of them left New York with little to their names, selling their possessions, clearing all debt, and doing everything they could to garner a fresh start. They visited Shakespeare's home as a kind of creative pilgrimage, a hat-tip to a younger self.

Bartering and hustling to get by, never having enough money, but no longer caring, AJ and Mel slowly grew their company, Misfit Inc. Before long, they had more than enough, but they continued the same nomadic lifestyle, slipping across continents like minutes slip through fingers.

I drain another cup of coffee, the rich taste sending a tingle up to the roof of my mouth. AJ and I have sat opposite each other for the last hour, exchanging stories.

"On the plane, I kept thinking about when I was younger, comparing myself then to how I am now," I say, running my finger over the edge of the coffee cup. "I used to be so committed to the task at hand. I would live it, you know? I was so busy when I started the business, between studies and everything else. I spent every moment focused and excited, committed to what was in front of me. But over the last few years, that excitement has drifted away, I guess. At times, it's like I'm on autopilot or playing a role, you know?"

AJ nods, lifting his own cup to his mouth. "I do," he says, looking past my shoulder and smiling. "You want to know the first thing I did when I received that offer from my boss? I walked into my office, closed the door, and cried. I looked out my window, over the Manhattan skyline, and cried.

"I felt trapped, and it was like it finally hit me. That was the moment I realized what kind of life I had been living. But this wasn't the first time I'd cried. Some nights, I would just break down and ball in front of Melissa, for no reason at all.

"Each day, I put on a costume of some guy named AJ Leon, who didn't look or act anything like me. I didn't know any of this, of course. I didn't realize it. I was living life and doing what I thought I had to, but there was always this friction between who I really was and who I was trying to be."

"That's it," I say. "That's how I feel. It's like I'm me but not. I wake up each day and leave the house to live this supposedly amazing life, but it's like I'm not the one living it. I meet so many people who tell me how lucky I am and that the world is at my feet, so I feel guilty the moment a negative thought enters my head.

"I mean, I should be happy, right? There is no reason I shouldn't feel happy. So I force myself into feeling it. I go out. I meet people. I drink. I stay out. I talk about how happy I am and what my plans are and how I'm going to become the next billionaire in Silicon Valley. It's what I'm supposed to do. It's what a guy in my position has to do. But it's like a different guy is doing all this. It's not me."

"But you can't express this," he says, smiling. "Because if you do, you're ungrateful and delusional."

"Exactly."

He nods, laughing. "It doesn't matter because if it doesn't feel right to you, it will never feel right. You can only kid yourself for so long, brother. You can only hide and put on that costume for so long, and that younger version of you, the one who was happy, who was himself, who did what he wanted . . . he'll never shut up.

"He's in you, and he's smarter than you give him credit for. There's a lot of wisdom in youth. When you're young and money doesn't really matter, you do things that light a fire within you. You're free, and you do what you like. That's what it was like for me. People assume I found myself while traveling, that I became this different person after I left my job. But all I really did was return to who I once was. I would do something that fired me up and I'd remember something from my youth that would make me feel alive.

"When you think about it, that makes sense because, when you're younger, you are the real you; it's a time before you inherit all the noise that society throws at you." He smiles wide. "It's like when you're sixteen years old, you're eighty percent you and twenty percent nonsense ideas. But over time, you get diluted, drop by drop, until you become a watered down version of the person you remember being. That's all I am today, a mirror image of sixteen-year-old me. Misfit, what we do and why we do it, is a mirror image of who I was back then."

I say nothing, weighed down in my chair, as life seems to sit on my shoulders. I nod. "It's not about finding something new. It's about rediscovering what you've lost."

"You've got it."

"So what should I do?" I ask. "How do you just change your life?"

He smiles, rubbing his bearded chin. "Don't wait. What you're doing right now, where you're thinking and ruminating on this . . . don't. Because this life is simple. We all have a certain amount of minutes, and those minutes are expendable. When they are gone, they are gone, and they're ticking away." He clicks his fingers with each word. "You are going to die, Ferdinand," he says. "You don't know when, but it will happen. You will die. You are here right now, but one day, you won't be. And that day could be today . . . tomorrow . . . any day! Do not wait. The fact we're having this conversation means you already know the answer. You know what you're doing isn't right, and you know you have to change. So do it. Do not wait."

I laugh. "But it isn't that simple—"

"Doesn't matter," he says. "It doesn't matter if you don't know what to do. If I told you that you had five days to live, would you be sitting here wondering what to do? Or would you go out there and do it?"

I gaze over his shoulder, to the outside world of passing-by bodies and lives ticking away, moment by moment by moment.

"Maybe there isn't a master plan," he continues. "Maybe all any of us can do is the next thing . . . and then the next thing . . . and the next. I didn't have a master plan when I left my job. I had no idea that I would end up here, speaking to you, or about any of what's happened between then and now.

"When I left, I was terrified. But at the same time, I felt free, truly free, for the first time in a long time. It felt amazing. Because who is free in this day and age? Do you have any idea what it's worth? I know people with so much money who are miserable because they feel imprisoned. By their business, their relationships, their responsibilities, the decisions they made years, sometimes decades ago. So few people are free, but during that period, I knew I had reclaimed my freedom, and I could not let go of it ever again."

I shake my head, heart racing. "But I cannot just let go of everything I've built. It's not as simple as quitting and leaving."

"Nothing ever is. This life isn't easy, but you are the only one in control of it. You want things to change? You have to change them. And the truth is, Ferdinand, it's easier for you than it is for most people."

"In what way?"

"You kidding me?" He laughs. "You have enough money and know enough people and know that you could come back and start again. Do you know what I had when I left my job? Nothing! I'd spent years earning good money and spending it all on stuff I didn't need. Mel and I had to start from scratch again, bartering and selling all that *stuff* just so we could travel here," he says, poking his finger into the table. "And when we got here, we had nothing and had to keep bartering just to eat.

"We had nothing, but we still had a choice. I chose freedom, and almost anyone can make that decision. But almost everyone comes up with the excuses you have in your head right now."

I close my eyes and sigh. "I know what you're saying, and I know you're right. But—"

"It's hard. It's scary. It's jumping off a cliff and hoping to grow wings before you hit the ground."

"Yeah," I say, drifting off and gazing over his shoulder once more.

"But I did have something you don't," he says. "I had Melissa. And if I didn't, I'm not sure I could have done any of it. She is the quintessential partner. I mean, she is the exact person you want by your side if everything around you is burning to the ground. She never made me feel bad. She never complained or lost faith in my decision. She was in it with me to the bitter end. She believed in me more than I believed in myself."

He stares at me, leaning into the table as he talks about the woman he loves. In an instant, I'm alone. I picture Beckie, how she's no longer here. She left me. She left me here, alone.

"If more people had someone by their side like Mel is by mine, more people would have the strength to do all this."

"I don't have that," I say quietly.

"Maybe you've not wanted it," he says. "Worse, maybe you had it but refused to let it in."

TEN.

Contollo's Boardroom, San Francisco

My chair creeks as I rock gently back and forth. I'm alone, though, only moments ago, I occupied this room alongside the other nine men who make up Contollo's board. There was a time when it was just me but then, more men—all older than me, most white and grey, suited with ties and polished shoes—entered the room. The boardroom table grew longer and more expensive while the chairs became less comfortable.

I look around. Everything is white and clean. White walls and white cabinets, glossy and reflective. If I were to break down my personality into a room, would this be it? How much of "me" is in here? Only the wall to my right feels at all personal; my friend, Wil, created the mural that fills the entire space. I recall his ideas and how I loved them. But as more of the board heard more of his plans, the less of his liberal vision made it onto his canvas.

Adrenaline continues to pour through me, my skin tingling after the last hour or so in here, breaking down my thoughts and frustrations. Ray mediated as best as he could. I didn't feel like me, but in part, felt truer to myself than I have in years. Returning, as AJ said, to a person I used to be, the man I planned to become.

I used to fight, stand my ground, and say what I felt. Over the years, drop by drop, the environment I've placed myself in has diluted me, more and more, as more and more cash entered my bank account. Money I don't use all that often, dollars I very rarely think about.

Yet it's all I strive for.

On the plane home, I'd thought about nothing but success and what it means to me, the supposedly successful man I am, and the money and fame. I thought of Jordan and his "why" questions, of AJ and his outlook on the "what."

"What is success to you?" I'd asked him as evening arrived.

He looked at me, sipping his bottle of beer. "I don't know. I have no interest in being successful; I know that much," he said. "I want to be significant, but I don't see that as having anything to do with success. I can be wildly significant and impact a lot of people, but that may never translate into success, money, or fame. I mean, what even is success? Is it a certain amount of money? Was it the job I had? Do I need to own a home or a car or live in a certain zip code? Or is it freedom? Does the freedom I have now mean I'm successful?" He leaned into me, a hint of beer on his breath. "Everyone gets hung up on success, but hardly anyone knows what success is. They follow a vague version that their parents created for them, or their friends, or the magazines they read, or the shows they watch. Success is too warped, but significance is simple. Am I significant? Am I impacting those around me? Do I have a positive effect on the world, even if it's just for a short time?"

We had talked for hours more, and beer transitioned into whisky. Time passed quickly, but the words have stuck. On the plane, during the ride from the airport, at home last night as I lay in bed after calling this emergency board meeting, throughout this morning, as nerves rattled beneath my skin, as I sat in this chair while those nine older, more experienced men walked through the door with curious eyes.

Success . . . what is it? Is it real? Does it matter? What does it mean to me, and what does it mean to this company?

My conversation with AJ awoke something, a deep and underlying feeling that had yearned for a voice for so long. It was a voice I had silenced, like an insecure teacher does the child who challenges them.

"Well, that was a disaster," Ray says, charging through the door and shaking his head. "Ferdinand, what was all that about?"

I look at the mural. "I hate that thing," I say, pointing at it.

"Hate what?"

"That. The mural."

"It was your friend who did it, so—"

"No. Wil had a great idea. I loved his vision. But the rest of you didn't. So I told him to change it. And you know what? I hate it."

He sighs, rubbing his hands down his cheeks. "Fine. But right now we have other things to talk about."

"That mural symbolizes everything I said in the meeting," I say, placing my hand on the table. "This is my company. I started it. When I did, I had a vision, a dream. It meant something, but bit-by-bit, I've listened to other people and gone along with them. Well, over the last few days, I've taken a step back, and I hate what I see. When I look in the mirror, I don't see me, and I do not like the guy who's replaced him."

Ray sits in the chair next to me. My heart races once more, as it did during the meeting. Going into it, I didn't know what I would say. Each time, I planned it in my head, but one thought would run into the next.

So confused.

So distraught.

"I just don't understand, Ferdinand," he says. "None of us do. We're growing. We're making more money than ever. We've just landed a huge round of investment, and plans are underway to go public. You're going to become a billionaire, and you're sitting here telling me you're unhappy. Do you know how immature and ungrateful that is?"

"No," I say, standing up. "It isn't. This isn't about money or market share. This is about significance and meaning. This is about making a real difference."

"And a billion dollars isn't enough?"

"It isn't about money," I say, taking a long breath and walking toward the window. "When I spoke to AJ, I kept talking about our plan for a billion users, going public, and becoming the latest hundred-billion-dollar company. How I would join the billion-dollar club. He just looked at me."

"Who cares about what he thinks?"

"I do. I felt embarrassed telling him about our grand plans. I realized they didn't mean anything to me. I thought they did. These last few years, I woke up and went to work, assuming they mattered. But they don't. They never have."

"Where is all this coming from?" he asks, shaking his head and puffing out his cheeks.

"From the beginning, Ray. Before you. Before any of this," I shout. "AJ said he cannot fathom what it would be like to serve a billion people. All he cares about is impact and significance. He would rather go a mile deep with a few than a few inches with many. When he said that, a younger version of me woke up. The guy who started all this in the first place."

I picture myself back then, passionate and animated each time I spoke to anyone about my mission to advance and refine how we communicate with each other in this hyper-connected world. "It's so inefficient," I'd preach, angry and frustrated. "All the email chains and DMs, it's such a waste of time. We need to communicate less, and I don't see anyone doing anything about it."

I feel the same anger and frustration rise up now, not just about how inefficient it all remains, but how I seem to have forgotten about the one thing that was once so important. "It's dawned on me," I say. "What are we doing? Why are we so obsessed with the word 'billion?' It never used to be the obsession. The obsession that got you involved—that got us the first ten million that made all *this* possible—focused on redefining how we communicate with each other. Remember how I told you about bringing all the tools you need into one place and intelligently bringing the right people into the conversation at the right time? That's what *hooked* you, Ray. We wanted to create less communication, not more."

"That's still the focus," he says.

"Is it? Why do we seem to create more and more features then? We keep giving our customers more, not less. Sure, it looks cool and sounds sexy, but is it really helping solve that problem that once mattered so much?"

He says nothing, just shakes his head. "So that's it. After one conversation with a stranger, your entire dream is done? You no longer care about going public . . . is that what you're telling me?"

I laugh. "It was never my dream, Ray."

"What is?"

I move to speak but hesitate. "I don't know. I've lost sight of it, and that's what I need to figure out."

He stands and joins me, leaning his shoulder against the glass. "We've been through a lot, Ferdinand." I look at him, his darkened skin and worn face, wrinkles spread across his forehead and cheeks. Sunshine pours through from the window behind, bathing him in light. "I want to be honest with you right now," he continues. "This is not how it works. You don't call a board meeting like this and try to tear down everything you've spent years building. These people have invested a lot into you. These people are older and know a lot more about business than you. You are lucky to have a group of people like this involved in your business. Do you know how many young startups would kill to be in your position?"

"Don't, Ray," I say, shaking my head. "I respect you. You're a great mentor, and you have done a lot for me. But don't tell me how lucky I am to have all this. I built this."

"This is the problem with your generation," he says. "You're so dang entitled. You've grown up in a world that gives you everything, protects you from everything, and makes you think you deserve everything. Guess what, Ferdinand, you don't. This isn't how it works."

"Is this really going to become a millennial-versus-boomer debate, Ray?"

"There is no debate. You're a smart generation but a spoiled and lucky one."

I laugh.

"You literally have the world at your feet, and you're willing to throw it all away." His face is tense, his posture more so. "This won't play out as you want it to, Ferdinand," he continues, his tone stern and short. "Those men have the power to force you out. Some of them already want you gone. They have for a while. They think we need a more experienced CEO. They see you as the *face* of the company and nothing more. But I've always stuck beside you. After this, though, I'm not sure I can."

"I know," I say, my heart sinking again. "It's one of the reasons I've felt so vacant of late. I guess I've tried to carry on, pretending like this is my company and that I still play an important role. But deep down, I've known what you all think."

"You're acting like a brat. Whatever happens, you're going to be a very rich man."

"This isn't about money, Ray. This is about being honest with myself, and figuring out if all this is what I want," I say, motioning my arms around me." You said it yourself, sometime soon we'll go public, and everything will get a whole lot worse."

"Worse? You're going to be a billionaire. How is that worse?"

"You know what I mean."

"No," he says, spitting out the word. "I don't understand. All I see is one of the most intelligent and talented young people I have ever met, who built something amazing, trying to sabotage it as it's about to become a success. I don't understand that."

I nod and smile. "Maybe it is a generational thing."

Huffing, he strides toward the table and leans on a chair. "What do you want to happen from all this, Ferdinand?"

"I'm not sure."

"No, that's not good enough. This is serious, and I need to know what you want. I can calm things down and give you some time to do whatever you need to do, but trust me when I say that they will come after you. And listen to me when I say this, I will not stop them. There are a lot of people involved in this company, and I will not let you ruin it because you've read a few self-help books and talked to a hippie."

I look down at his shoes, memories of trips to the principal's office coming to mind. "I'm not sure what I want. I just know I don't want to feel like this. I can't keep coasting like I have these last few years, and I can't—"

He grabs both my shoulders. "Ferdinand, what do you want?"

"This is my company. This is my life." Tears swell in my eyes, out of nowhere. "I need to get away from all this and figure out if *this* is what I want."

He sighs and purses his lips, placing his hand on my arm. "Okay. Calm down. It will be okay. I've always trusted you. From the moment we first met, I believed in you, and I will continue to believe in you . . . for now. But you're digging yourself a hole here, son. If you're not careful, the walls will cave in on you. Everything you've built . . ." He sighs. "Everything we have built, they will take it away."

ELEVEN.

First Class, Somewhere Over The Midwest

The dull roar of the plane's turbines is all I hear as I block out my surroundings and focus on a half-filled champagne flute. Untouched for over an hour, the initial taste was not as crisp and refreshing as I've found it in the past. Much of what I used to find refreshing no longer is: food, drink, clothes, people . . . this large first-class seat, with all its extra legroom and space and comforts; it's supposedly luxurious but still cramped and claustrophobic. I'm high above the ground, hurtling through the sky. I'm not in control of this situation, the pilot is. A stranger locked away in an unseen cabin. The air is still fake and chilled, as it is in the other classes.

I used to take pictures and share them online, gloating about the mile-high Wi-Fi. It all seemed so important. The bubbles in the glass are few, the drink flat. Christian is seated to my left, though I only see his sprawled legs tapping a rhythm, lost in his music, I presume. We haven't spoken since we sat down. I've yet to speak to anyone, nodding and avoiding eye contact with the flight attendants.

I'm trapped in a metal tube with hundreds of other people, heading toward the middle-of-nowhere Ohio.

Five weeks have passed since the board meeting and that chat with Ray. A brutal few days followed, as I was called into meeting after meeting. The board wasn't happy. People were worried. They all wanted answers. Everyone had an opinion—most not favorable.

I'm insane. I've had a crisis. I'm a spoiled brat. I will regret this.

It soon died down. After a few days, their minds focused on other problems, other opportunities, and other ways to fill their days. I got the feeling that most, if not all, warmed to the idea of me leaving, were excited by it, even.

Even Ray seemed to make peace with it.

"I've bought you three months," he said. "I'll keep everything at bay until then, but after that . . . I'll be frank with you, Ferdinand, most of them want you gone." He said this without spite or malice, just indifference, as though passing on a message from someone he bumped into at lunch.

My emotions have ridden a roller coaster since, especially as I lay alone in bed. Beckie's memory is long gone. She left and she isn't coming back. We haven't spoken since, and I don't sense a time soon when we will. Still at night, I roll over and think of her. Thankfully, during the days, I've been kept busy with meetings and strategy sessions and plans to ensure I pass everything I need over to someone in some department.

But on my own in that giant house I'm so pleased to leave behind, my mind hopped from one emotion to the next—excited, but scared; relieved, yet stressed; ready for the chance to escape, though crippled by the thought of what may come next. I may have lived in denial in recent years and coasted through life, but at least I knew what each step was. I woke up with an agenda. I had places to be, people to meet. I had a business to lead, even though I now realize I didn't do a great deal of leading.

What happens now?

I embark on this adventure in the hope of finding something, a solution. But what if I don't? What if I only find more questions and more confusion? What if all this leads to me losing my business, only to have nothing to replace it with?

"You okay?" Christian asks, snapping me out of my nervous trance.

"Huh?"

"You okay? You need anything?"

"I'm fine. Just thinking."

"A lot of thinking," he says, leaning against the back of the seat in front. "I suppose I shouldn't complain, seeing as I'm getting to tag along." He smiles, sipping from his glass of champagne.

"Someone has to look after me."

He laughs. "True. And seeing as the first stop is to visit Wil, I'm not sure you would get out of that one alive on your own."

My turn to smile.

"I have to ask," he says, leaning closer. "Why Wil? I don't exactly know what you're expecting to get from this soul-searching trip, but you won't get much from him, surely."

"You may be surprised," I say. "There's something about him that's . . ." I search for the right word. "Unique."

"He sure is unique."

"I know he's a bit out there, but he seems to have gone through a lot over the last year. He's changed, seems different. I don't know what it is exactly. I guess that's why I want to speak to him."

"Well, just be careful," he says. "As attractive as he and his English accent are, he's crazy. He actually reminds me of someone my sister dated back in high school, and—"

"Wait," I say, cutting him off. "You have a sister?"

"Yeah."

"How didn't I know that?"

"I'm pretty sure you did. I've definitely talked about her."

"I don't remember you ever mentioning a sister."

"Well, I don't see her often. She lives in New Zealand. But I've definitely mentioned her before. In fact, I'm sure you met her when she came to visit a couple of years ago."

I squint, searching my mind for a time he mentioned her, when I apparently met her.

Nothing.

He shakes his head. "Maybe you changing isn't such a bad idea."

A voice comes over the speakers, informing us that we're about to begin our descent into Dayton International Airport. Christian settles back into his seat, muttering something as he does. I buckle my belt and stare out the window. Streaks of white above and below, us sandwiched between them, flying and falling.

That's me, flying forward into the unknown but falling all the same. That's me, sandwiched between my past and future.

TWELVE.

Wil's House, Dayton (Ohio)

Wil assures me he's lived in this house for over a year, but it seems like he's yet to move in—beige walls are completely bare; two simple chairs sit empty with a small table between them; a record player is stashed in the corner, a crate of vinyl next to it; another larger table hugs the opposite wall, with little on top but a bottle of whiskey, a few glasses, and a white stone statue of Marcus Aurelius, I think.

No pictures or artwork; no TV or speakers; not a couch or rug or pillow in sight.

I didn't realize how empty this room was when we arrived last night. We headed out almost immediately, grabbing food and a few drinks, walking around the sleepy town. Students were always close by, backpacks over shoulders and notebooks in hand. It was quiet, a far cry from the metropolitan busyness of San Francisco or New York.

"Tell me again why you live in Dayton," I ask, as he enters the room with a tray of coffee and cups.

"Ferdinand, m'boy, you will love this coffee. The best I've come across, bar none. Love it, I say." He dashes to the table, spins around, and eyes me. "How about we transform these coffees into something the Irish would appreciate?"

I laugh. "Sure."

"Good man, good man . . . And Dayton? Why, yes, I do live here, and I do have reason. Helps me focus, you see," he says, splashing whiskey into each cup. "The town I grew up in, back in England, not too different from this place."

"I thought you hated that town."

"Hate? Oh no, m'boy. Not hate. Outgrew, yes. But far from hate. Plus, too many ghosts and demons back there. We all need to run from time to time. But I find we often return in some form. This sleepy little town is familiar, yet different. A nice balance."

I take the cup of coffee and hold it to my nose. Strong fumes rise, a mix of dark bitterness and smooth single malt.

"Will Christian be joining us?" he asks.

"Not for a few hours—has some work to catch up on." I bite the corner of my lip. "I sense me leaving has made things rather chaotic for him."

"I see, I see. Yes, I imagine so," he replies, fidgeting in his seat.

I recall meeting Wil for the first time. I assumed he was high, seeming to dance along with his words and starting his next sentence before finishing his last. He never seems able to settle on what he wants to say or get the thoughts out of his head.

"This journey you're on . . .I'm excited for you, m'boy. The exploration. The ascension up the mountainside. The exhilaration you'll soon feel. So very exciting."

"I'm not sure I share your excitement. I feel more confused than ever." I look around the room once more. "Speaking of confusion: What is up with this room? It looks like you've just moved in. Why do you have nothing in your house?"

"Ah, nothing is not what fills this room. Everything in here has a purpose, and everything that didn't is no more. No distractions. No extra vanities that exist only to make me feel better about myself. Does a TV allow me to appreciate me? Does art on my wall help me create my own? Does a library of books I'll never read make me wise?"

He scoots his chair closer to mine. "Ferdinand, I have stayed in your home. It's beautiful. It's the envy of many. You have beautiful things all around you, but how much of it do you notice? If I were to ask you to name all the items in your living room, could you? What about that kitchen; have you used every plate? What about your bedroom, and its closet; have you worn each item of clothing until it's comfortable?"

I sip more coffee. "No."

"Like so many, my friend; like most. I was like that. But ever since I removed clutter from my life—the items I didn't need, the tech I didn't use, the thoughts and beliefs I clung to—I feel more free, more focused."

"I suppose that makes sense," I say. "Consume less so you can appreciate more."

"Exactly," he says, sitting up straight and pulling a coin out of his pocket. "That's it, m'boy. Well said, well said."

He stands and walks to the record player, flicking through the vinyl. "I came across these two chaps, Ryan and Joshua: the minimalists. They wrote a wonderful book and created a rather nice documentary. They had the high-paying jobs. They earned a lot of money. They had enough, but rather than enjoy what they had, they continued to fill their lives with more.

"More, more, more, that's all we ever want. We chase and strive for more, and we so rarely stop to ask why. But if you strip away the excess in your life, you're left with nothing but your thoughts." He smiles, removing a black record and placing it on the player.

"You certainly seem to have a different outlook from the person I once knew," I say.

He smiles wildly. "I suppose I stared down the barrel of the gun, much like you've done of late." He comes back to join me, as The Cure plays in the background. He flips the coin in his fingers, fidgeting with it and rubbing it between fingers.

We spoke at length last night, over dinner and then through drinks. We talked about me, this journey so far, and the feelings I've felt of late. He said little, sat and listened, and took it all in.

"Have I ever told you about my very good friend, Dante?" he asks, looking at the silver coin, pinching it between finger and thumb.

"I don't think so."

He says nothing, stares at the coin. "He was my best friend," he says quietly. "The best of friends and, in all honesty, the only person I have ever truly trusted. I grew up with him, and, no matter what happened, he always stood by my side. I'm not sure why . . ." He drifts off. "He died a few years back. Terrible cancer. Stole his brain and his body with it. So young for such a tragedy, and even though I knew it was coming long before the day arrived, I couldn't quite believe it when I got the call to say he was gone. Have you ever lost someone you love?"

I shake my head.

"Terrible. It still hurts today. I think of him every day, and I hope I always will. But all the same, I sometimes wish the memory of him would vanish." He places the coin on the table, looks at me. "I went off the rails when he died. And that's saying something because I lived life somewhat off the rails while he was alive. But when he did die, a part of me went into the darkness with him.

"I didn't show it on the outside, of course. I traveled and lived life, slept with women week after week, drank, took drugs . . . did anything to help me escape." He shakes his head. "I didn't enjoy a second of life. Even though the pictures I shared online told a story of me living it to the fullest."

He leans forward, perches on his knee, and points a finger at me. "One day, I woke up and felt different. Not sure why. I was in Bali, and I had spent the previous day like the many days before it. But something awoke inside me on this particular morning. And I felt peace." He stands and takes a few steps away from me. "I sat on the beach and looked out to the sea, thankful to be alive. My friend wasn't, you see. He wanted to be. He had a wife at home and a son he never met—a little boy I couldn't bring myself to look at because all I could see was the friend I missed so dearly. He had so much to live for, but he couldn't because he was gone, and he would never return." He strides toward me, settles back down on the couch. "I crumbled into pieces as I sat in the sand because I knew I lived without any care for life. I drifted through the motions, wasting the seconds I was given, devoid of emotion. I looked down the barrel that morning, m'boy. I wanted to cry, but I couldn't. I didn't want to waste another second of life. So I left Bali later that day." He stands again, walks back toward the bottle of whiskey. "Last night, you spoke a lot of success and purpose and meaning. I suppose it was on that plane home that I started to muse over such things for the first time. Until then, my life had been nothing but a game. I rebelled out of the fear of being like everyone else. I rebelled against my father, school, and society because I was afraid I might fail to meet their expectations.

"I acted like nothing and nobody could affect me; yet I would spend each night lying in bed, worried about what other people said about me." He leans against the table, seems to look through me. "Not long after, I met you and all those successful people you know so well. I liked how you lived. I wanted to be like you. So I buckled down and committed to the *hustle and grind*, as you Americans say.

"It worked, too. I quickly found some quote-unquote success. Yet I still felt empty inside. It was all still a lie. Hanging around with fine folk like yourself did nothing but distract me from the infernal racket going on inside me. Just as I had while traveling, I did anything to quiet that voice. Until, one morning, I woke up to a familiar song."

He picks out a record. Holds it up. "You know of Death Cab for Cutie?"

I nod.

"There's a song on this record, 'I Will Follow You into the Dark.' I've only visited Dante's grave once. I went with his cousin and wife. The three of us stood there, looking at a chunk of stone that represented his life as I sang this song and played the guitar, and . . ." He doesn't finish the sentence. "Anyway, this one fateful morning, I woke up with a hangover from the devil himself, and what played over the radio but this very song. Out of nowhere, I cried. I don't mean the odd tear running down a cheek, either, m'boy. Uncontrollable sobs erupted out of me. I couldn't stop it." He hands me the record and sits down. "I decided there and then I would finally face it—what I was running and hiding from. I had no idea what *it* was, but I knew the time had come to finally stop running. So I left San Francisco and moved to Dayton. I remember speaking to a fellow Brit named Sam in New York a few years back—a music producer, I think—he told me about how his best friend lived here. 'Sleepy and boring,' he had said. As soon as I arrived at the airport, it was the first place that came to mind. Sleepy and boring is exactly what I wanted." He picks up the coin, continues to stare at it, and twirls it between his fingers. "That's why I'm here. I bought this house with my so-called success, sold my possessions, and rid my life of as much baggage as I could."

"Then what?" I ask, barely a whisper.

"I began to search for *it*," he says, pointing to the record in my hands. "Each morning since, I play this song and look in the mirror, make a promise to myself—and to Dante—to live a life worth living today. No focus on tomorrow. No worry about what others may think. Just a promise to live today."

Silence engulfs us. I look at the record, the black-silhouetted crow wrapped in red string. I hear my heartbeat, the heavy thud within. "I'm sorry, Wil. I had no idea."

"Why would you, m'boy? It isn't something I talk about. But I think about it each day. I try not to fight it anymore, like I once did. I wake up and listen to that song and think of my friend. I make a promise not to live a successful life but one of meaning. Just today . . . Just focus on making today the best it can be. What more can you ask for?"

I say nothing.

"Everything else is white noise, Ferdinand. We fill our world to the brim in the hope of filling the many voids within. That isn't success. I have no idea what success is, but I'm sure that isn't it." He places the coin on the table and slides it toward me. "The man who gave me this coin helped me realize this. When I first met him, I was not ready for him. I had my eyes closed, caught in the San Fran hustle and grind with you and your pals. I had to stare down the barrel of that gun for some time before I was ready to open my eyes." He purses his lips and takes a deep breath, seeming to push a thought to one side.

"Who was it?" I ask. I look at the coin, notice for the first time that it has a triangle cut out of its middle.

"I don't know his actual name. He goes by *Turndog.*" He stands quickly, rushes toward the record player. "But this new outlook of mine—the one you highlighted earlier—much of it's down to him and his ways. He helps those that seem successful actually feel successful."

"Like a coach?"

"No, no," he murmurs, shaking his head. "Not a coach. It's hard to say what he is, but he's had a huge impact on me. He's introduced me to a great deal, but it's all built atop of something ridiculously simple: *letting go.*"

"Letting go of what?"

He smiles that wide grin of his. "All of it, m'boy. Everything you can."

THIRTEEN.

Bus Stop Cafe, New York City

"Maybe we're born with it," Wil said to me at the airport. "Maybe that *it* we yearn for is within us, somewhere deep below those layers of distractions we've built over time. That's why we're blind to it. That is why our eyes are closed. Over time, we place all these layers over them: beliefs, false truths, ego, rules, possessions . . . and we cover our eyes, until we're unable to open them. This is why we must let go. We need to let go of it all so we can see once more." He held me firm by both shoulders and smiled, wearing a bright white fedora, a navy blue tweed jacket, and pinstripe trousers. "I am excited for you, m'boy. You're ready to let go. Soon, you will see." He hugged me and dashed off, skipping across the shiny floor and out the airport doors.

That was two days ago. We had talked and walked, and I found myself forgetting about the chaos of recent weeks. I felt myself letting go–*of the worry, the confusion, the relentless questions swirling around my mind.* Still, I have no idea what I'm looking for. The *it*

Wil spoke of remains invisible. It's frustrating. I keep trying to let go of it, relax, and let what will be, be. Yet the frustration is there. I feel it, fuelling those endless questions.

I raise my cup of black coffee to my lips—still warm, no longer hot. The bitter taste lingers on my tongue as I close my eyes and breathe deeply, inhaling the rich aroma. I open them and look at Christian, tapping away at his keyboard, face half covered by the screen. He suits a coffee shop like this. Like everyone in here, he has a sense of effortless style, an *edge*.

I don't. I'm too clean cut. I didn't used to be. Back in college, I had an *edge*: more unkempt, baggier clothes, longer, more styled hair.

I *had* an edge. Past tense, no more.

"What do you expect will happen from all this?" I ask Christian, rubbing my hands up my face.

"What do you mean?" he replies, eyes still on his screen.

"This trip. This, whatever it is?"

He stops typing. "I have no idea. I was hoping you might know that."

I sigh. "Do you think I'm crazy?"

"Do you?"

"Maybe."

He looks behind me, in search of the right words to use, possibly. "I'll be honest, I thought you were. I figured you had reached some weird quarter-life crisis and that this trip would last two weeks. But after going to see Wil, I'm not so sure. Like you said, he seems different, in a much better place."

"He is. Different from the guy we knew back in San Francisco, right?"

"Yeah. He always seemed a little lost to me, as though he was trying so hard to be accepted. But now, he seems more at peace with whatever the heck goes on in that head of his."

I laugh. "I think that's one of the problems I've been having."

"What?"

"Being okay with who I am and what I have."

"I don't get that," he says, sliding his laptop to one side. "You have everything. I can see why someone like me might be dissatisfied with where I am, but you're a multimillionaire with the world at your feet. What more do you want?"

I sink into my seat. "I don't know. That's the problem. I feel guilty feeling this way. Like you say, I have everything anyone could ever want. But I do feel it. And as I look back on these last few years, I feel like I've been living life on autopilot, on a mission to become a billionaire and take the company public. But is that what I want? Once I do that, will I be happy?" I sigh. "My mind won't settle. All these questions, ideas, and feelings are spinning around in there." I continue, tapping my forehead. "It's exhausting. I want answers. I just want to stop feeling like . . . this."

"So what's next?" he asks. I sense his frustration, too.

"I don't know. Part of me thinks this whole thing is a huge waste of time. Wil kept saying to let go, but how do you let go of a soon to be multi-billion-dollar company? How do you change your life like that?" I push my knuckles into the sides of my tender, aching skull.

"Do you remember Matt Bodnar?" Christian asks after a few seconds of silence.

"Yeah."

"I remember talking to him once about how people fall into the trap of living black-or-white lives. That you have to choose either one or the other, whereas, in truth, there's usually a lot of grey in-between. It kinda sounds like that's where you are at the moment: stuck in an either-or outlook.

"Yeah. Maybe."

"He's based in New York. I can call him if you'd like? May be a good person to talk to."

I rub my chin, the three-day-old stubble coarse against my fingers. "Sure. Good idea." But I have no idea what a good idea looks or sounds like anymore. My mind continues to abuse itself, half-thoughts and incomplete sentences crashing into one another.

I have a headache. Everything seems to ache. "What am I doing?" I whisper into my cupped hands, pushing them up my face and through my hair. I look up at the ceiling, high above and way out of reach. A fan spins fast, so fast it seems like it doesn't spin at all.

FOURTEEN.

Wilfie and Nell's, New York City

I watch her cross the room, from the bar to the bathroom, decked in yellow with a bright red scarf. I recognize her face but can't quite place a name to it. I used to always remember a face. I took great pride in the fact. No matter who I met, I'd take careful interest in their name, associate it with their face, and lock it in my memory. I no longer do this. I meet too many new people; their names slip through me like the drinks tend to. I search my memory for hers. Nothing. I sigh, furrowing my brow and sipping from my glass of whiskey and a little ice.

The bar is lively, with a constant background of chatter and music that makes hearing the person across from you difficult. Matt sits opposite me, his back against the bare brick wall. I sit on a bench, my neck and shoulders tense. The woman I may or may not know reappears from the bathroom. She doesn't see me, smiling as she passes and walks toward her group.

"Sorry about that," Matt says, placing his phone on the table. "It sounds like you've been asking a lot of questions recently," he continues.

I don't recall when we first met. A friend of Christian's, he came to some event at some point. We got talking, the usual back-and-forth. He invited me on his podcast, and I unleashed my usual spiel that always seemed to work, until I met Jordan, of course.

"I can relate to AJ," he says. "I know what life on Wall Street is like and how easy it is to lose yourself in the pursuit of corner offices."

We're on our second round, and I sense a third on the horizon. I've brought him up to speed on my recent weeks. My interview with Jordan, the trip to see AJ, my talks with Wil. He's sat, sipping and silent. I've talked, sipping and sad. I don't know why, but I feel down, lower than I've felt in as long as I can remember.

"I worked on Wall Street," he continues, "surrounded by people living unconscious lives. I was one of them. I had my eyes closed, walked through life asleep. Most people do. Not just in a place like Wall Street, either—most people, period. They live on autopilot, careening from one experience to the next, without stopping to think whether they want to experience it."

He looks around the room, shaking his head. "It's sad to think, but most people don't escape this. You need to stumble across someone who stops you in your tracks and pulls on a thread, shows you there's another way."

"Who was it for you?" I ask.

"This guy I met while I did my training. We kept in touch afterward, and I noticed how successful he had become. He was my age but had written a book and kept getting featured in magazines. He seemed to be doing much better than I was. So I figured

I would ask him how he did it. He gave me a thread to pull." He smiles. "I pulled it."

"Then what?"

"Life, I guess. I read the books he recommended and found myself stumbling down a rabbit hole of new ideas and questions. There was no purpose to it . . . I was just curious. It's the only way a journey like that can begin—take a first, daunting step and have the humility and curiosity to learn."

I nod, relating to the daunting steps into the unknown. "So you got the answers you wanted?"

"Some, I guess," he says. "But not all of them. And that's okay. You don't need all the answers. Just the curiosity to keep pulling the thread."

I massage my forehead with fingers and thumb, neck stiff and head heavy. "I feel like I'm holding on to a lot of threads at the moment, no idea which one to pull. I should be happy and grateful for all I have, but—"

"You're not," he says.

I nod again.

"You've just described most people, Ferdinand. They feel like they should feel something but don't. They should feel grateful or successful or happy, but there's this inner voice that never stops. It's hard; it's exhausting."

I nod again, adding a sigh.

"So tell me, what's the one constant feeling you feel at the moment?" he asks.

"There are a lot."

"I'm sure. But I imagine there's one that stands out, one feeling that always seems to be there?"

I hold in a breath. "Frustration," I exhale. "I'm frustrated I feel this way, that I don't have the answers, and that I don't even know what questions to ask. I'm frustrated my girlfriend left me despite giving her a good life. I'm frustrated at my board for not appreciating me and trying to push me out of my own business. The business I built. I'm just . . . frustrated."

"Yeah, I sense your frustration," he says, grinning and drinking. "What about fear?"

"Fear?" I ask.

"Yeah. Fear. What are you scared of?"

"Who said I was scared?"

He smiles. Warm, without judgment. "You've tipped your world upside down. You're pulling on all these threads. You telling me you aren't scared?"

"I don't think so," I say, my neck tighter. "What I'm doing is brave. It's hard to walk away from everything I had. Everyone thought I was crazy. There's a lot going on up here," I say, tapping my head. "But fear isn't part of it."

"Yeah?"

"Yeah," I snap, my tone harsher than intended.

He smiles again.

"Sorry," I say. "I'm a bit on edge today."

"I sense that, too." He laughs and drains his glass. "Does the idea of fear put you on edge?"

"No. I just think people glamorize it," I say, my tone still short. "You can't let it stand in your way. If I did, I wouldn't have gotten to where I am today."

"So you do feel it?"

"That's not what I said—"

"You don't let it stand in your way," he says, cutting me off. "But you still feel it."

I sigh. "What's your point?"

"My point is it's okay to be scared. What you're doing right now is scary. Building the kind of business you are and trying to balance everything is scary, too. It would be insane if you weren't. A lot of frustration is born out of fear, but you don't face it, so it hangs below the surface."

I take a deep breath, notice the room around me: the people, the music, and the incessant noise.

"What are you scared of?" he asks.

"I don't know."

"You sure?"

I exhale and look down to the worn wooden floor. "What if I'm wrong? What if all this is a massive mistake, and I spend the rest of my life regretting it?"

"Regret what?"

"Walking away from it."

"Have you walked away from it?"

"I feel like I have."

"And you're afraid of losing it?"

"Yes, although part of me wants to, I think." I shake my head. "I'm torn. On the one hand, I have everything I could ever want. There's this voice, telling me to go back and appreciate what I have, that to walk away from it would be the biggest mistake I ever make. That I should work with the board again and just follow through with the plan. Yet I have this other voice, reminding me why I started Contollo in the first place. Shouting at me to stop because things are way off course."

"Why did you start it in the first place?"

"To advance and redefine how we communicate with each other. To create less communication, not more."

"And that's not what's happening anymore?"

"No. Maybe. I don't know." I roll my eyes, conscious of the nonsense escaping me.

"Okay, okay," he says, holding up his hands and smiling. "Let's say it did all end. It's taken from you, or you decide it isn't what you want anymore. How bad would it be? Do you not believe you could build something else? Would the end of Contollo mean the end of you?"

"No. I could start again. I know I could, but . . ."

"But?"

"I don't know." I let out a deep breath and close my eyes. "I can't figure it out. It's all a mess up here," I say, pointing to each temple.

He shifts in his seat, leans toward me, and grabs my shoulder. "Life isn't black and white, man," he says. "Just because you fail doesn't mean you're a failure. Just because you walk away from one success doesn't mean you can't build another. Just because you're not the best at something doesn't mean you're the worst."

"But I've always been the best," I say. "Always the smartest, always the guy destined to achieve so much."

He says nothing but looks at me for a few seconds. "That's the problem for a lot of people," he finally says. "We're brought up to succeed and to fear failure. We're told to avoid mistakes and be good and kind. Scarcity gets programmed into us at a young age, so we form the belief that if we're not one, we're the other. Our brain's a meaning-making machine, creating stories and narratives out of everything, so it can make sense of the world.

"I have to take from them, or they'll take from me. I have to be the best; otherwise, I'm not a success. We subconsciously form these beliefs based on what we see and experience, and a lot of this happens at a really young age. It's how we learn. The problem is a lot of these beliefs are flawed, and they stay with us for a long time. They create a lot of fear around failure, being wrong, looking bad, what other people think of us, or not being enough, both to ourselves and other people."

"But this world is cutthroat," I say.

"Is it?"

"Yes," I say. "People are greedy. It's full of people who want to take from you."

"That's one way of looking at it," he says, settling back into his seat. "But is that really true?"

"Yes," I say with an assured tone.

He nods. Then smiles, warm once more. "It's that scarcity mindset. Where life is one or the other, black or white. It doesn't have to be like that, though. You have a choice. You can choose to have an abundant outlook, where we can help one another, where we don't need to worry about losing out because there's plenty to go around." He leans further toward me, cupping his hands. "Instead of the pie remaining the same size, we can grow the pie so everyone gets a larger piece," he continues, moving his cupped hands apart.

"It's a nice way of seeing the world," I say, folding my arms across my chest.

"But you don't agree?"

I let out a long breath. "I'm not sure."

"Have you ever read the book *Mindset* by Carol Dweck?" he asks. I shake my head. "It's one of the books that helped me. Before I read it, *mindset* was just a word. I didn't really understand what it meant. But this book showed me there's a lot to it, and that there are these two main types of mindsets: fixed and growth.

"A fixed mindset says you are either good at something or not. You see other people's success as a threat. Failure means you're no good, so it's better to quit and focus on what you're good at and avoid all that hurt. But a growth mindset says you can grow. Failure is a chance to learn and get better. If you're not good at something, you need to practice and progress. Another person's success is no threat, rather a chance to learn from them. There's a lot more to it, of course. The science behind it is fascinating. But this book is what sparked something inside me," he says, snapping his fingers. "It's why I started my podcast. I wanted to see how truly successful people approached life compared to everyone else."

"And the people you interview—the successful ones—they have a growth mindset?" He nods. "But you think I have a fixed one?"

He shrugs. "Maybe. Most people do. We only know what we know, and we go through life without questioning it. It's not like we get taught this stuff in school, is it? We just live life, until one day, we stumble across someone who gives us a thread to pull."

I glance at the mirror to my left, notice how straight my spine is, shoulders tense and raised high toward my neck. I close my eyes and breathe. "I think that's where I am."

He smiles and taps his glass. "Well, that's cause for celebration, if you ask me."

"How so?"

"Because all this begins with an awakening," he says, shifting in his chair. "Everyone is asleep until someone comes along and nudges them awake. Most people don't want to wake up. It's easier to go back to sleep and continue to live the life they know."

I think of my dream, the way I awake each time, sweaty, lost, panicked.

"I sense you won't, though."

"Why's that?"

"You wouldn't be here. You're questioning it. You're already in too deep. You're ready to take that daunting first step." He winks and slides his empty glass toward me.

"Yeah," I sigh. "A lot of questions but no answers."

"Maybe that's what you're afraid of," he says. "Maybe that's why you're so frustrated at the moment. Maybe you've always been the guy with all the answers, and for the first time in your life, you don't have them."

"Same again?" asks the bartender. I nod and slide him our two empty glasses, clear my throat and eye the shelves behind him.

Whiskey and rum fill the top shelf, with all other liquor below. On either side of the shelves is bare, brick wall, lit with old, industrial light bulbs. A long mirror hangs above, angled so it catches the top of my head and looks down my face as I look up to it.

"Here you go," he says, handing me two new glasses of twelve-year scotch. These are our fourth, the third having gone down as quickly as the others. Matt and I have continued to talk, diving deeper into mindset, what it is, and how it affects so much.

It's a word I knew of but never truly understood. I still don't. The idea that we live our lives imprisoned in a state of mind we have so little control over, many of our beliefs forming before we're old enough to speak is wild. How do any of us achieve anything if this is the case?

"Ferdinand Foy?" asks a voice to my left, leaning on the bar and catching my eye.

The woman I may or may not know from earlier stares back, her curly black hair covering half her face.

"I thought it was you," she continues, holding out her hand. "It's Ishita. We met at one of Seth's book launches."

I search memories, sifting through events and faces. "Yes," I say, biting my lip. "Ishita Gupta, right? You run a . . . magazine?"

"Yes," she says, smiling. "I'm impressed. Although I no longer run the magazine. On to new projects these days."

I nod, draw the two glasses closer to me as I turn to face her. "Would you like a drink?"

"No. Thank you. I'm actually with a few friends. But they're leaving soon, so if you're here a while longer, I'll come and say hello."

I hold up both glasses. "I'll be here a while yet."

"Great. Enjoy your whiskey." She quickly hugs me before I have a chance to react, sending a cold shiver up my spine before she steps back and rejoins her group. I think it's the first contact I've had from a woman in weeks.

I walk toward the table where Matt sits alone. He's told me about his own beliefs and how he realized they impacted him so much, for so long. Reminiscent of AJ, he lived a life he thought he had to live.

"I realized I had created an entire narrative without any conscious awareness of having done so," he said. "This had formed over twenty-plus years and ruled how I lived. I had to step back and question this story and ask why certain thoughts crept forward in certain situations. Only then could I uncover what was really going on.

"I began to see how scared I had been and how I thought I had to beat other people. If I wanted to climb the ladder, it had to be at the expense of someone else." He looked at me, shame in his eyes. "I didn't like it. I didn't want to be that guy. So I've spent my life since distancing myself from him."

He'd talked more about mindset and the fundamental differences between a fixed and a growth one. At first, I related to the growth outlook. I've always focused on coming up with solutions, never allowing adversity or setbacks to hinder me.

Yet the more Matt talked, the more I related to the fixed outlook, haunted by scarcity and fear.

Fear. Am I scared right now? What of? Why?

"Thanks," says Matt, taking a fresh glass of the good stuff.

"So, what's different for you today?" I ask. "When you compare yourself to who you were, what's changed?"

He smiles. "Everything. When I first began to question things and realized I wasn't happy with who I had become, it felt like I had woken up. Everything has changed since then. How I start my day and how I continue it. How I think and act and react. Work, health, relationships . . . there's nothing it doesn't touch." He leans his elbows on the thick wooden table between us. "Do you believe you've woken up?"

I nod. "Maybe. I think so. I don't know"

"What do you need to do next?"

"I have no idea. I'm hoping you can help me with that one." I smile, a little drunk.

He laughs, sips from his glass. "I can't help you with that. It's your journey. And even if you are awake, you may not be ready to see just yet. It can take time for your eyes to adjust to the new day." He smiles, seems to laugh at himself. "It's a long journey, man. I'm still on mine. I catch myself drifting off back to sleep most days."

"What do you mean?"

"Negative thoughts, scarcity, a black-and-white outlook. It's all still there. It doesn't disappear because you're suddenly aware of it. Your limiting beliefs don't vanish because you start to question them."

"But there has to be some kind of . . ." I rub my eyes, trail off into silence.

"What? A guide? A blueprint? A roadmap you can follow?"

"Sure."

Another laugh, a larger sip this time. "Afraid not. There are entire philosophies built around this stuff but no rule book that tells you what to do and when."

"But there has to be—"

"Why?" he interrupts.

"Why what?"

"Why does there have to be a solution?"

"How do you overcome it otherwise?"

He places his drink on the table and leans closer. "It isn't black or white, Ferdinand. There's no award at the end of all this. No promise of riches. No round of investment or an invite into the billion-dollar club. This is about you living your life the way you want to live it. It's your choice. If you want to go back to sleep and carry on the way you've always lived, go ahead. There are no rules, man. Only the ones you create for yourself."

I squeeze my eyes shut and grit my teeth. "But that's so frustrating. You see that, right?"

"I know."

"It's too big of a risk. How will I know if all this is worth it unless I know what I'm getting myself into? What if all I do is make things worse?" He shrugs his shoulders. "Back home in San Francisco, I know what I have," I continue, frustration bubbling out of me once more. "I have a life and a thriving business and money and fame and anything I want. But out there," I say, pointing to nowhere in particular. "What is it? What will I find?"

"I don't know." He smiles. "Nobody does. You're standing at a crossroads, and you get to choose whether to take the leap or go back to sleep. There are no guarantees either way. This is just you choosing how you want to live your life."

I rub my face and sink into my chair, weighed down with whiskey and indecision.

Matt stands and drains his glass then picks up his jacket and sliding his arms through. "I know it may not seem like it, but where you are right now is a good place to be. Whatever you choose to do next, you'll be better off for having questioned all this." He shuffles to my side of the table, phone in hand. "I have to make a quick call home, but a final whiskey before we head out?"

"Definitely," I say. "I definitely need one more."

He places a firm hand on my shoulder and walks off, leaving me alone at the table once more.

I sip from my glass, holding the harsh taste in my mouth. Not yet drunk but getting there. I close my eyes and take a deep breath, trying to calm the chaos within. My head seems to dance along with the background music I can barely make out, soothed by the liquor that always does its job so well.

"You look like a man with a lot on his mind."

I open my eyes, greeted by a large smile. "Hey, Ishita."

"Is it okay if I join you?" she asks.

I motion to the chair. "You need a drink?"

"I'm good," she says, raising her nearly full glass. "Everything okay? You seem a little lost in thought."

I smile, lips slightly numb from the whiskey. "It's been a crazy few weeks."

"I imagine they all are when you're a billionaire."

"I'm not quite there yet," I say.

"I'm sure it won't be long. You were so focused on it the last time we spoke."

"I was?"

"It's all you talked about," she continues, smiling so large her eyes almost vanish.

"Oh." I rub my temples, dulling the ache with tiny circles.

"Are you sure everything is okay?"

"Yeah. Well, I don't know. Like I say, it's been a crazy few weeks."

She says nothing.

"Can I ask you something?" She nods. "Have you ever questioned everything you were sure you knew was true?"

She smiles again. "Oh, Ferdinand." Her smile turns into a laugh. "Almost every day."

FIFTEEN.

Central Park, New York City

There's a chill in the air as I take a long breath in. I hold my arms close and rub my palms against each other. The air is crisp against my skin, though not biting. It's refreshing above all, as I close my eyes and take an even longer, deeper breath.

I hold it in my lungs as I look around, up to the lush, green trees and out toward the light blue lake.

It's been a while since I last came to Central Park. I'm not sure I've ever been to this part of it, though I understand why Ishita insisted we meet by this particular lake on the Upper West Side. Ripples spread out and into one another, lapping gently and mixing with the hushed sound of the breeze and awaking birds.

It's early. Too early, the sun only just making its ascent into the sky.

I cannot remember when I last woke at this time, at least not without a plane to catch or a meeting to rush to. I hated mornings as a teenager and have insisted since that I am not a morning person. Yet when I do rise as the sun begins to, I always feel calm and refreshed, as though the early morning light washes the previous night away.

All colors are pale–the sky and lake, trees and clouds. In a few hours, the sun will help each hue stand out, but for now, everything remains understated. I hold in another breath, my lungs tingling. My eyes tingle too, still adjusting to the day. It wasn't a late night but far from an early one.

Matt had briefly returned to join Ishita and me at the bar, soon leaving so he could spend time with his wife. We plan to meet for lunch, Christian joining us this time around. I thought about everything he had said while I drifted off to sleep. I thought about Ishita, too, and her reaction as I'd brought her up to speed with my recent weeks.

It's becoming scripted, me saying the same things in the same order, as if spewing out a speech to a potential investor. She sat silent and smiling as I told her about the interview with Jordan, my escape, and the journey since.

"It's interesting you say escape," she said. "Is that how you feel?"

I didn't know how I felt. I still don't. *Is this an escape? If so, what am I escaping from? What do I expect to find?*

She soon finished her drink and insisted I meet her here, at this time. "The water is beautiful, and the park will be so quiet. You'll love it."

It's hard to disagree, leaning on a tree and gazing at the shore. The city skyline peeks over the treetops, revealing the concrete jungle that exists beyond nature's edge. The sounds of cars and city life are there in the background, but those awakening birds drown them out, that and the lapping of water against dirt and rock.

"Good morning," comes a familiar voice from behind. "Sorry I'm a little late."

"It's okay. Just enjoying the view, as you said I would."

"You've been here before, surely?"

"To Central Park, of course. But here, I'm not sure."

Ishita stands beside me, bundled up in a bright orange jacket. She looks out to the lake, closes her eyes, and smiles. "I always forget how much I love this time of day. It's so calm and crisp."

I nod. "Do you always get up this early?"

"No. I always say I will, and I often intend to. But it's easy to forget how much I love this when I'm under my covers, and it's cold outside." She cups her hands and breathes into them. "So how are you feeling?"

"Tired."

"Other than that. What's your heaviest feeling right now?"

"What do you mean?"

"Your heaviest feeling. What's weighing down your heart at this very moment?"

"That's a deep question for this time of day."

"The perfect time to ask it," she says. "Go on, what weighs you down? There are always many but usually one that underlies the rest."

I smile. "Matt asked me something similar last night."

"I can see why. You seem like you have a lot on your mind. It gets overwhelming, doesn't it?"

I nod.

"So what did you tell Matt?"

"Frustration."

She nods. "You seemed frustrated last night. Where's that coming from?"

"It's like you say, there's a lot going on at the moment. It's overwhelming, and I'm frustrated I feel this way."

"You're frustrated at feeling frustrated?"

I laugh. "I guess I am."

"So where is it coming from?"

I sigh and bundle my hands into my pockets. "Matt seems to think I'm scared."

"What do you think?"

I catch her eyes, notice how dark they are. "I guess I am scared."

"And how does that feel, admitting it?"

"I'm unsure. It makes me feel uncomfortable because I'm not used to saying it."

She begins to walk, motioning me to follow. "So where does that come from? The fear?"

"I guess I'm torn. Part of me feels proud of doing what I'm doing, as though I'm in search of something better. But another part of me feels like I'm making a massive mistake and will regret this for the rest of my life. I'm on this sabbatical, but what am I doing? Am I really going to find anything, going from city to city, speaking with people?" I shake my head. "It feels like I'm hoping to stumble across a solution to all this."

"So, where's that feeling coming from?" she asks. "Why do you feel torn? Why don't you feel like you've committed to this journey yet?"

I puff out my cheeks. "I'm not sure. Matt thought—"

"This isn't about Matt," she says, cutting me off. "This is about what's weighing you down. Here you are, at sunrise in Central Park, on a beautiful spring morning, surrounded by all this," she continues, raising her arms. "Yet you're so tense."

"I am?"

"You look like a guy in mourning."

"I feel like I am," I reply. "This business has been my whole life for so long. What if, at the end of all this, I decide to walk away?"

"I imagine it would be hard."

"Exactly. I'm torn. I don't want to feel like I have these last few years, but I also don't want to lose everything I've built."

"That's tough," she says, swaying slightly as she walks. "But what if everything you've built so far is a stepping stone to more?"

"What if it isn't?"

She smiles and arches her brow. "I guess you'll never know, which is hard. Not having that control is scary when you're used to having so much of it."

"Control?"

She nods. "You've always had a plan. You have always been the best at what you do, right? You have been in control the whole time, but here you are, unsure about what's ahead. Maybe you'll realize Contollo is the business you've always wanted, and everything will be fine. But maybe you won't. Maybe you'll have to start again; maybe you won't be the best anymore." I say nothing and simply take in her words. "Does part of you feel guilty?" she asks. "Shame, even?"

"Shame? What do you mean?"

"Well, you should be happy, right? You have everything you ever wanted, but you're not happy. It should be easier for you now. You've done the hard work, and now is the time to enjoy it. Plus, a lot of people have looked up to you, relied on you. You can't let them down."

"Shame," I whisper. "I hadn't thought about that," I say, louder. "Maybe. I've always felt like I had it together. While everyone else wondered what they would become, I knew. As everyone else asked questions, I had the answers."

"You made a lot of people proud?"

"Sure."

"You feel proud about what you've achieved?"

I nod, the breeze whipping past my ears.

"Yet here you are, possibly ruining it all."

"Yeah," I sigh, stopping and looking up to the tree above. The greens and blues beyond it are stronger now, less faded and washed-out.

"So, where do you think all that comes from?" She asks, stopping beside me and nudging my shoulder.

"I don't know."

"Maybe that's where you need to look. Because after everything you've achieved, should you feel this way? I'm not sure you should, but you do, and that's fine because you feel it for a reason. It doesn't make you weak. The most successful people I know aren't devoid of fear or shame. They're as human as anyone. They're just aware of what they feel, and they look at why they feel the way they do."

"Then what?" I ask, a sense of frustration rising within, as it did last night when I spoke to Matt. "I search for it. I ask why. I go see a therapist and analyze my past . . . then what? What happens after that?"

She shrugs. "I have no idea. But maybe you can start giving yourself a break. After all, you're a pretty cool dude who's achieved more than most people ever will. You've gotten through life so far on the back of your talent, persistence, and charisma. But maybe these same strengths are now what hold you back."

I face her. "But I know I've achieved a lot. I'm not an idiot. I'm aware of my successes, and I know where I've come from."

"Sure you are. The problem is, there's this battle between rational you and emotional you. Rationally speaking, you know you're good and talented and have what it takes. But, emotionally, maybe you feel like you haven't done enough, like you're not good enough."

I say nothing, looking beyond her and toward the buildings jutting high above the green leaves.

"What's your relationship with your parents like?"

"And there's the question," I say, shaking my head.

"What question?"

"People always try to make it about your parents, don't they?"

"What people?"

"I don't know. Shrinks. People like that."

"Well, I'm not one of those."

"You sound like it." She arches her brow. "Sorry," I say.

She winks. "What I mean is, were your parents supportive when you were growing up? Did they take an interest?"

"Yeah. They were really supportive."

"In what way?"

"The usual way parents are. They would reward me when I did well. They turned up to my football games and science fairs and took an interest in what I was interested in. They were proud of me. They pushed me to always give my best."

"Okay," she says, smiling. "So they were supportive. But only as long as you were achieving something?"

"I don't know about that," I reply quickly. She says nothing. I take a deep breath and picture them both, standing side by side, hand in hand. "Okay, maybe they did always focus on the end result. But aren't all parents like that? Everyone wants their kids to achieve straight *A*s and be the best they can be."

"True."

"So, what are you getting at?"

"Think about it for a second. When you're a kid, all you want is love. It's built into our DNA, to survive and feel secure and safe.

It's all we need as an infant, and it's basically all we need until we're old enough to look after ourselves. So for years, all we do is focus on the things that make us feel accepted, safe . . . loved."

"So, if your parents only make you feel like you're worthy when you win, all you focus on is winning," I say, more to myself than to her.

"Exactly. Emotionally, you feel like you have to be the best and achieve something huge, otherwise you won't get the love and affection you crave. But even if you reach it and build something amazing, you feel like you cannot stop. You have to keep going. To build something bigger and better because if you don't, all that love and acceptance will get taken away." She pauses. "My parents, they loved me. I knew they did, but they rarely told me. So, I spent most of my life pursuing my mother's approval and because I only got it when I was near perfect, I developed huge insecurity and self-doubt.

"Intellectually, I knew I was smart and good enough, but I didn't believe it emotionally. I spent years trying to prove myself to other people, to myself. I struggled to trust my decisions and ideas, so wouldn't commit to anything. No matter what I achieved, it was never enough because I never felt like I got the acceptance I needed. And even if I did, I feared it would get taken away from me as soon as I stopped being perfect. This is why I started FEAR.less. I knew I shouldn't feel this way, and I wanted to overcome it. So I started a magazine about overcoming fear and self-doubt because it's something I needed to do. I wanted to trust myself. I wanted to appreciate who I was. And I soon realized how many people struggle with this, and how important it is to not only figure out who you are, but understand *why* you are," she says, raising her hands with a flourish.

"There's a reason why you do what you do, Ferdinand. You're not some messed up human being who acts randomly. There's a reason for all of it, and I'm not saying it's your parent's fault. I don't know one way or the other. But neither do you, and until you do, you'll remain at war with yourself: *rational you versus emotional you.*"

My eyes tingle. I'm unsure why. The cool breeze strokes my face but not hard enough to bring about tears. Yet I feel them. I sense them awakening in each corner, ready to break free and trickle down my cheek.

"It works the other way, too," she continues. "Rationally, you know how amazing the life you've built is. Money, fame, power," she says, raising a new finger with each word. "To become a billionaire is to achieve so much that you will always feel safe, loved, and accepted. You will be forever enough." She approaches a tree and leans against it. "But maybe, deep down, you're unhappy with something. Emotionally, you fight it because it doesn't feel right, but rationally, you fight back because you believe it should feel right."

She laughs and looks out over the lake as the sun begins to reflect into it. "It really is exhausting. I lived like this for so long, pushing myself and trying to prove my worth, but never feeling . . . enough."

"So what do I do?" I ask.

"That is the question."

"I'm serious, Ishita. I hate feeling this way. What can I do to figure it out?"

"You're doing it, dude. You're beginning to question it."

"Sure, I know . . . but what did you do? How did you overcome it?"

"This isn't about what I—"

I cut her off. "There must be something you did that I could do?" She says nothing. In the silence, I realize how tense I am: shoulders, back, neck, even my fingers are wrapped up into fists.

"You're trying to force it," she says. "This isn't a meeting with an investor. This is you going up against you, and right now, your rational self is pushing for an answer. You won't find it like that."

"So what am I supposed to do?" I ask, closing my eyes and running my cold hands over them.

"Be kind to yourself," she says, placing her hand on my arm. "I've learned the best way to approach any of this is with love and kindness. I know that sounds a little woo-woo, but it's true. Self-love is the biggest piece of this puzzle. You cannot bully yourself into changing. Trust me, I tried. It didn't work."

"But loving yourself did?"

"You bet. You want to know why?"

I nod.

"Because self-love is where you merge who you were with who you want to be."

SIXTEEN.

Ferdinand's Apartment, New York City

> *Love . . . I promise you that the same stuff galaxies are made of, you are. The same energy that swings planets around stars makes electrons dance in your heart. It is in you, outside you; you are it. It is beautiful. Trust in this, and you and your life will be grand.*

I close the book and rub the matte-covered cover with my thumb. I turn it over and look at its cover: *Live Your Truth.*

It was written by Kamal Ravikant, a guy I do not know but with whom I now feel a kind of intimacy toward. I had never heard of him until Ishita mentioned him during our walk, insisting I read his book about loving yourself. I ordered two of his creations while we walked through the park. They arrived the next day.

This morning, I opened the first. *Love Yourself: Like Your Life Depends on It.* I anticipated a few minutes of reading as I drank my first cup of coffee. But before I knew it, I had completed it and reached for *Live Your Truth,* reading that cover-to-cover, too.

It's been a while since I started and finished a book in a single sitting. I used to do it as a teenager, wasting away entire Sundays with Kerouac, Hemingway, or Fitzgerald. It's rare I read at all these days, let alone lose myself within the pages like I just have. I made notes and underlined passages. Something else I used to do: not only read a book, but immerse myself in it.

I flip through the pages, the paper fanning my face, noticing the sentences marked in red pen.

Pain doesn't last. And when it's gone, we have something to show for it. Growth.

Sometimes the only way to evolve is to open ourselves fully. Be raw, honest. Vulnerable.

"One thing I've learned: we don't stumble accidentally into an amazing life. It takes a decision, a commitment.

Love, pain, fears, hopes, dreams, desires. All arise from the mind. We're stuck in heads, walking around, reliving old stories and patterns and beliefs.

This one reminds me of Ishita—stories from her own past, and how they impacted the way she lived. How she couldn't trust in herself, despite knowing she should. Feelings, that's all any of it is.

"I am most valuable to others when I love myself," she told me. "I am at my best when I love myself." She smiled, those eyes almost vanishing once more. As I read Kamal's words, I heard much of the same.

Peace is letting it be, letting it flow, letting emotions flow through you.

Whatever ego you've developed, look hard at it. You will find aspects that no longer serve you.

The best people, they're afraid, they question themselves . . . But what separates them from the rest is that they jump off the cliff anyway. Sprout wings on the way down.

This one reminds me of AJ—taking the leap.

Maybe Ishita's right. Maybe a battle rages within me, stuck between wanting more and yearning to feel . . . enough. Has the fine line between ambition and presence blurred the lines between my reality and dreams? What dreams do I even have anymore? What is it that I want? Have I only ever yearned for safety and acceptance, assuming achievement and success would bring it?

Is this the same place I've turned to for love?

Love. I'm not sure I've ever taken the time to feel it. As a kid, I'm sure, when it was all I needed. But since infancy turned into adolescence, I can't recall a time I've thought about it. Too busy to love myself, too focused on what comes next, what my next challenge should be. My parents loved me. I knew they did. I always knew it was there, but they embraced and encouraged my excellence. Why settle for less when you can commit further and become the best. Anything less than that is weakness, right? And if I'm weak, I'm at the mercy of failure. And if I fail and don't bounce back quickly, I'm no longer in control, no longer good enough.

So to love is to be weak.

I look once again at the front cover, the bright white text against the dark background. I feel a heaviness inside me—not sadness, but shame. All the women who tried to enter my life, who I kept on the outside, looking in. I wanted them for what I wanted them for but no more. I figured I gave them what they needed in return: excitement, fun, money . . . *stuff.*

I close my eyes and picture Beckie. She left, but did I give her reason to stay? She loved me, and I said the words to her, but did I feel them? Believe them? Did she ever believe me when I said those words to her? Opening my eyes, I look at the blank wall, notice a smudge of dirt on it, stare at it, and focus on what I'm feeling. The heaviness, the shame, the emptiness. I don't feel sad, though. I feel like I should, but I don't. If anything, I feel a strange sense of hope.

"To change inside," Ishita said to me, "you need to be easier on yourself. You need to show love and compassion."

I have a choice. If I'm unhappy with the way I've been, I can change. If I want to be someone else, I can. If I want to let others in, I will. I have a choice. It's all we ever truly own. I look below the smudge of dirt to the table under it. Kamal's other book rests on it. I pick it up, rub my fingers over the glossy cover. *Love Yourself: Like Your Life Depends on It.*

"I have a choice," I whisper.

The door swings open and Christian rushes in with a grocery bag in each hand. "That's something I haven't seen for a while," he says, dropping his load next to the kitchen counter. "I can't remember the last time you read a book."

"Neither can I," I say, passing it to him.

"You always used to have a book in your hand."

"I know." I walk to the kitchen counter and sit on a stool. "I always carried a book with me growing up. At school, I must have read at least two each week."

"Too busy to read these days, I guess," he says, unpacking one of the bags.

"Maybe." I pick up a banana and look at it. "I used to read because I loved it. I enjoyed escaping into a different world. But then it became about the books I *should* read," I say. "All those textbooks and business books, the latest bestseller everyone raves about."

He nods, opening a bag of pita chips. "Yeah. Once you've read ten of them, you've read them all." He crunches a few chips between his teeth. "So how about this one?" he asks, clearing his throat and looking at the book's cover.

"Amazing."

"Yeah?" He picks it up, flips through the pages. "You've made notes. Must be good." He smiles. "So do you?"

"Do I what?"

"Love yourself."

I peel the banana and shake my head. "I don't think I do. But after reading it, I have a feeling most people don't."

He flips through the pages again, chewing chips and licking his lips.

"Have you ever been in love?" I ask.

He stops, looks at me with surprise. "Once. Maybe."

"Maybe?"

"I think it's hard to know for sure. I didn't feel butterflies every time he was around me. Nothing like that. But I did feel like I was missing something when he wasn't there. I suppose that's love, right?"

I laugh. "I have no idea."

"You've never felt it?"

I shake my head. "Who was the guy?"

"Remember Jeff?"

"Yeah, blonde and preppy."

"That's the one."

"What happened? You stopped feeling it?"

"No. I felt safe around him to the end. I missed him a lot when he was gone, but we just lost that spark. We became friends more than anything."

"Do you still think about him?"

"Sure. Sometimes."

"I keep thinking about Beckie."

"Yeah?"

I nod. "I've been angry at her. She left me. I had given her so much, but she decided it wasn't good enough. She said she loved me and believed in me, and I guess I had tricked myself into thinking I loved her. That what we had was love."

"But now?"

"After reading these books, I kinda get why she left. What we had wasn't love. In the beginning, it was exciting, I guess. But then it just became a relationship of convenience. At least, it did for me. She wanted more. She wanted love. But I suppose I was okay with what we had. I was getting what I needed from it."

"But she wasn't."

I shake my head. "It's how I've treated all the girls I've dated. I feel bad about that, yet at the same time, hopeful. I get to make a choice, you know? I don't have to be like that in the future. I might not be able to change what I've done, but I can choose what I do next." I take another deep breath and smile. "It's kinda exciting."

"That does sound exciting," he says. "What about Beckie? Do you think you'll speak to her?"

"I don't know. Not now. In time, maybe. I always wanted to love her, I think. But I never did."

He nods, looking at the book. "I think I need to read this."

"You should. We're going to meet the author in a few days."

"We are?"

"Sure. Once you find out where he is." I wink at him, walking away, feeling lighter and more hopeful than I have in a long time.

SEVENTEEN.

Burgos, Spain

The paved stone floor glistens, wet from the recent rain and aglow in the sun's light. The sky remains grey, although patches of blue peek through. It's calm, quiet. A few people walk through the square, flanked in all directions by buildings rich with time.

I've been to Europe before. Many times.

I've walked through the streets of Paris, Rome, Prague, and London. I've come here for business. I've come here for pleasure. But like so many things in my life, I appreciate now how much of it was for show.

I have looked at the buildings rich in history but not seen them.

I've taken pictures and posed in front of them but haven't taken the time to feel them.

I do now.

I'd never heard of Burgos before speaking with Kamal and learning that this is where he is. It took Christian a few days to track him down. I called but met his voicemail each time. I left messages and sent texts, and then received short, dismissive replies.

Two days ago, he finally answered. "Who's this?"

I told him. A few seconds of silence. "Oh, okay. What can I do for you?"

I told him how I'd read his books and loved them, said I would love to meet him and talk. I'm used to people saying yes, excited to meet me and grab a drink. He hesitated, countered with, "Maybe." I recognized his tone as the one I often use with people I'm in no hurry to meet. "I'm in Spain at the moment. No idea when I'll head back to the States."

"I could come to you," I said. "Where are you?"

"Burgos."

"Where?"

"It's great. I'll be here for a few more days, so if you want to come, I'm happy to meet you, though I'm in-between books so not interested in talking about business or investment."

"That's okay," I said. "Neither am I."

The next day, Christian and I were back on a plane. He updated me with messages from Ray. He keeps trying to arrange a call with me, but I continue to dodge and avoid the possibility. I know I should talk to him. I need to at some point. Yet the mere thought of it makes me nervous. The business I built from nothing is way over there, being run by other people, with me playing no role. In part, I want everything to be running smoothly, yet another part of me wants to see it burn to the ground; to show people need me; for those on the board who want me gone to realize the value I bring. I fear the former is more likely than the latter, and the thought of Ray confirming this sends my stomach in knots.

After Christian finished telling me what I supposedly needed to know, I read Kamal's latest book, *Rebirth*. A fable, it follows a lost young man as he travels the Camino de Santiago. He passed through Burgos, and I suddenly realized why Kamal is here. It was a journey he took himself as a younger man, in-between his own Silicon Valley successes.

We have several friends in common. He's an angel investor and startup founder but unlike most I've met before. Through his words, I felt his pain, his confusion. I related to his stories. I suppose it's why I'm here, sitting beneath a parasol as raindrops drip on my bare toes. I'd woken early and walked through the streets. On the plane, I promised myself I would spend some time with myself. No pictures. No social media updates. No shops or tourist hotspots. No Christian.

Just me, taking in what I see. The old, narrow streets. The aged, bricked buildings. The bright, colorful roofs. The rich tapestry of windows and doors, each with their own unique stamp. Everything in this town is so lived in. There are buildings older than the America I know. I've never stopped to notice how incredible that is.

There are steps that were trodden by men and women hundreds of years before me. Bricks laid by a worker in his prime, who's lain buried for generations since. Stone that's gone through a hundred seasons of rain, ice, snow, and sun.

To me, I'm everything. My life is all-important and all-encompassing.

But to this town, I'm a mere blip, a few thousands steps lost among a trillion.

"Ferdinand, how are you?" Kamal asks, snapping me out of my daydream. "Been here long?"

"Not sure," I say. "Just been enjoying the view. Nice to meet you," I continue, rising to my feet.

"Same. I need the bathroom and definitely a coffee. You want one?"

I nod as he vanishes into the cafe's shadows as quickly as he arrived.

Ten minutes later, he dips fresh bread into his black coffee. A few strands of his long, grey hair flop over his eyes. He has a youthful face, devoid of wrinkles or stress. To see him from behind, you would assume an old man awaits. But as I look into his face, a seemingly younger one than my own peers back.

"So," he says, clearing his throat. "Why are you here?"

A few minutes of small talk seems to have been enough. "I liked your books," I say.

"You flew all the way to Spain because you like my books?"

"I don't have much else to do at the moment."

"Ah, yes. I heard you're on a sabbatical of sorts. How's that going?"

"I'm not sure. I don't think I've found the answers I'm looking for, yet. I guess that's why I'm here."

"For answers?" I shrug. "I have none of those."

"I don't know about that," I say. "Your books, they—I relate to them. You're a good writer."

"Thanks."

"The whole idea of loving yourself . . . I hadn't really thought about it before. Too busy pushing myself and searching for perfection," I say with a smile. He just stares back. "So, I guess, I would love to learn more."

"About loving yourself?"

"Yeah."

"Okay."

"So how do you do it?"

"Do what?"

"Love yourself." I laugh. I'm unsure why.

"That's your question?" I shrug again. "Perhaps be more specific. Ask me a question I can answer."

"Well . . ."

"It's a broad question, you know? And people who ask broad questions get broad answers. But you can't apply a broad answer. You need to be specific."

I close my eyes and take a deep breath. "I'm not sure I have anything specific to ask."

"Then why are you here?"

"I'm not sure. I guess I just want . . . answers."

He sighs and bites off a chunk of bread. "Who doesn't? It's a mistake most people make. They think they want the answer, but the real answer tends to be more incisive and rarely gives them what they need. Because to get a real, clear answer, you need to ask a real, clear question. People don't ask good questions," he scoffs, sipping from his coffee. "Most people don't even ask a question. They just expect an answer." He arches his brow and smirks.

"Sounds like me," I say, the coffee cup warming my palms. "It also sounds like you have people ask you this stuff a lot."

"Sure. I don't blame them, though. I don't blame you for wanting answers, either. I've been where you are. Many times. When you feel pain, you want to overcome it. You want someone to help, to solve it for you. But you know it doesn't work like that.

"I can tell you my story. I can talk about how I learned to love myself. But what's the point? You've already read about it. I can't tell you any more than what's in those pages. Besides, what worked for me may not work for you. Most likely it won't. I don't have the answer you want. You have to go out there and live it for yourself. That's all any of us can do."

"Well, I'm here, aren't I?" I say. "I'm living it. At least, I'm trying to."

"You can't try to live life. You just do it." He shakes his head. "It sounds like you're traveling from country to country, meeting different people, expecting them to give you *the* answer. But what's your question?"

I smile. "Am I doing the right thing?"

"About what?"

"My business. My life . . ."

"Too broad. Be specific."

I laugh again, more relaxed now. He smiles, rips another piece of bread off like a lion tears through its prey. "How did you do it?" I ask. "When was the point you realized you didn't love yourself, that there was a problem? When I read your books, I felt your pain and confusion. I could relate to it."

"That's another mistake people make," he says, swallowing. "They look for a specific point in time to focus on. They want a *thing* to grab onto, to say, 'That was my tipping point.' That isn't what I experienced. There was no single moment or person. Life's too nuanced for that. It's a mosaic. Your mind is a tapestry of life already lived. Everything that has happened already happened. It all comes together to form your journey, so trying to pick out a certain moment to pin all your hopes on is pointless."

"So, there isn't a point you look back on and think, 'That's when it changed for me?'"

"Of course not," he says, dropping his bread to the table. "Anyway, that isn't the point. You can't dwell on the past. We're all messed up from it. Nobody gets taught to love themselves. Were you? Because I wasn't. I never even questioned it. I just got on with it. I worked. I started a business. I figured I would find happiness in success.

"Like everyone, I searched for answers. But I didn't ask the right questions. So I got frustrated. I got scared. I felt lost. What you read in my books . . . that's what it was. Me pushing for an answer, desperate. But I never stopped to think what question I wanted to ask."

"What was it?"

"What? The question?" I nod. "It doesn't matter. It wouldn't help you. You have to get out there and live your own life. Experience it. Sometimes you have to hit rock bottom before any of it makes sense."

I lean on my elbows and roll my eyes. "Sounds promising."

"I told you, I have no answers. Although, I will say this," he continues, clearing his throat. "If I could go back, I'd tell myself to not care about anyone else and what they think. It's where so many issues begin. We're insecure about everything, which is part of being human, I guess. But other people? They don't matter. What they say to you, what they say about you? It doesn't matter; they do not matter. Your only job in life is to make yourself better than you currently are. That's it. Make yourself better. Nothing else."

I laugh. "So, forget everyone else and live happily ever after."

"I don't know about the happiness part, but the longer you care what other people say and think, the longer you'll feel like you do now. My guess is you're terrified of what other people think of you. You've just turned your back on the company you built. What will people think of you? You're insane, an idiot, going through some sort of life crisis?

"What will people think if you don't have a successful business? What will people think if you fail? What if you don't live up to their expectations?" He shakes his head, more animated now. "Come to think of it, questions I wish I had asked myself a lot earlier are, 'What do I think about myself? What am I willing to do for me?' This is all you can control. Until the day you die, this is all you've got."

I consider his words, sit upright, and breathe deep. I've always thought I didn't care what other people think, but maybe I do; maybe I always have. Maybe I've always been trying to prove something to someone.

"Yeah," I say, sighing. "Screw everyone else."

He grabs my wrist, leans over his coffee. "Nobody can love themselves if they're obsessed with whether other people love them."

I nod, removing my hand from his grasp and raising my coffee to my lips "Can I ask you a question?" He nods. "You went on the Santiago de Camino, right?"

"A long time ago, yeah."

"Did it help?"

"Sure. But not because it's some magical pilgrimage, like most people presume it is. I've found I learn a lot when I travel. I like to explore. Traveling opens my mind." He leans back in his chair, picks up his bread once more. "Our brains weren't designed for this modern world. It's too overwhelming. I find traveling slows it down."

"I'm beginning to see that."

He nods, ripping another mouthful of bread off. "What you're doing is good. You're getting out there and living. That's all you can do. But that answer you're searching for? Nobody has it for you. It doesn't matter who you meet or how many people you speak to. All you can do is live your life, experience it. Along the way, maybe you'll figure it out. Maybe not. Either way, it doesn't matter."

"I need to figure it out, though."

"Why?"

"Because I've built this massive company, and everyone has these expectations."

"Screw 'em."

"I wish I could."

"You can, and in a way, you already have."

I smile. "Yeah. I guess I have."

"And let me ask you," he continues. "Those expectations everyone has back home, do you share them?"

I breathe and consider his question. "I'm not sure. I thought I did. But I don't know anymore."

"Maybe that's because, for the first time in a long time, you're starting to ask a few questions," he says. "Rather than doing what you're supposed to, you're questioning what you want to do. That's good."

"You think?"

"I don't know. You shouldn't care about what I think either." He laughs and stands, pushes his chair under the table, and leans on it. "So, what's next for you?"

"I have no idea. I guess I came here hoping it would lead me somewhere. Pretty stupid, huh?"

"No. That's not stupid. That's living it."

I say nothing, look beyond him and out into the square. The ground is mostly dry now, with a few wet patches scattered across it like spilled paint.

"You ever been to Cambodia?" he asks.

"No."

"It's a good place to go when you're trying to figure out what comes next. I was thinking of going myself, to do some writing. You up for it?"

"You mean, come with you?"

"Sure, why not?"

I say nothing, unsure what to say.

"I have no answers for you. Neither does Cambodia. But it's a good place to explore and live a little. From what I'm hearing, that's all you have to do with your time at the moment." He places a hand on my shoulder then disappears into the cafe.

I continue looking out toward the square. People are passing by in every direction. "Cambodia," I say. "Why not?" I lean back in my chair and finish my coffee.

EIGHTEEN.

Koh Rong, Cambodia

I twirl a little umbrella between my fingers—a spiral of color blurring my vision. Golden sand extends beyond that, and an almost-dancing blue ocean reaches out for forever. Sunshine rains down, though we are hidden amongst the shadows of the bar. A colorful concoction of alcohol splashes inside my glass as I twist it slowly in my hands. I have no idea what's in it. I don't care. It tastes delicious.

Kamal sits to my right with a bright cocktail of his own. Wearing a white, linen shirt and tatty, blue shorts, he looks out to the horizon, too. We haven't said anything to each other for the last ten minutes. In truth, we haven't said much in the two days we've been here.

On a whim, we left Spain a few hours after Kamal suggested it. Christian loved the idea, having visited Cambodia a few years ago. He booked the flights and sorted out the accommodations, and the next day, we were here. But since we arrived, we haven't done much, other than walking and sitting: in a bar, on a beach, on the deck of our wooden hut, overlooking the infinite blue.

We've talked a little. We've drunk, a lot. Not much more than that.

I continue to gaze across the bar, take in the people I do not know: a guy with a tanned, wrinkled face; a woman in a tie-dye shirt, her dreadlocked hair bundled into a ball on top of her head; a woman in a t-shirt that reads, "I Trust You," swaying from side to side as she sips from a long glass of something.

I glance back at Kamal. I feel cautious around him. I want to ask him questions, lots of them. But I hold back, as I sense he won't answer any of them. "Bad question," he keeps saying. "It doesn't matter."

I try to enjoy the silence and the peace, but I'm not used to it. I feel like I'm sitting here waiting for something to happen. I've never had the patience to just sit. I find the answer. I come up with a solution. Yet I keep coming back to what Kamal keeps saying—that it isn't the answer that matters but the question.

"What was it like, losing your company?" I ask, tired of the silence and my own relentless thoughts.

"It was painful," he says. "Ending anything is. A business. A relationship. A life. There's always pain."

The barman walks past with a towel over his shoulder. "I'm scared of that," I say.

"Of what, exactly?"

"Of it ending. Of the pain. I'm not sure I can handle it."

"Why?"

"I don't know."

He motions to the barman, holds up two fingers. "Fear is a natural state," he says. "Everything brings up fear. Anything you want or desire will bring it up. There's nothing wrong with it. You just have to recognize it."

"Then what?"

"You always want an answer, don't you?"

"Yes." I smile.

"What do you think the answer is?"

"I guess you just move on from it. Trust it will pass."

He nods, drains his glass empty. "As soon as you start something new—a business, a relationship, a journey like the one you're on—you understand it may one day end. But you start it anyway because you know how powerful starting something is. You will learn. You will grow. You will feel alive and energized. The fear is there, but you do it regardless because you know the only way to grow is by stepping outside your comfort zone." The barman arrives, places two drinks down, and walks away. "There's pain in starting anything. Ending something is painful, too. Everything in-between. But you do it all anyway. We either learn for ourselves, or life does it for us."

I nod, knowing he's right. "I forget which one of your books it's in," I say, reaching for my new drink. "There's a quote I like . . . something about how you're not the outcome, only the effort you put in."

"Sure."

"I guess that's part of it, right? To not place all your focus on the outcome, to just enjoy the journey."

"It's good to have a goal," he counters. "Whether it's a business, relationship, or whatever else, it helps to know where you're going. But it doesn't need to be specific. Yet people get lost in the details. They create a really specific goal, obsess over it, and build their entire life around that one, single outcome.

"If they reach it, they're left asking *now what*? And if they don't, they feel like a failure. So although you need direction, you don't need a specific point that defines who you are and what you achieve."

"Okay," I say, sipping my drink. "So I'm too invested in my business. If it fails, or I walk away from it, I feel like a failure. I define myself by how successful the business is and whether I become a billionaire or not. It means, whatever happens, I'm unable to enjoy the journey because I'm too focused on this single outcome." I take a deep breath. "Which doesn't even matter. Is that right?" He shrugs. "Oh, come on. Give me something." He smiles. "Fine," I sigh, laughing to myself. "I imagine it's less stressful, not anchoring yourself to an outcome."

"Sure. It gives you time to enjoy what's around you."

"I guess it's easier to love yourself that way, too?"

"Yeah," he says. "But look, it's not like you suddenly love yourself—just like that, nirvana. You're still human. You still get angry and frustrated. Some days you wake up and hate yourself. You still have doubts and insecurities. But you're kinder to yourself. You're no longer defined by this one single *thing*. It's easier to let it go and move on. That's love; that's kindness. We all know how to be kind and loving. The issue is, we often struggle to show it to ourselves." He leans toward me. "Take Christian. You care about him, right?"

"Sure. I've known him a long time. He was the first person I ever hired."

"Right. So let's say he makes a mistake and comes to you distraught. He's beating himself up and acting like he's a huge failure. How would you respond?"

"I guess it would depend on the mistake, but I'd tell him it's okay. Mistakes happen."

"Of course you would. Because that's how we treat other people we care about. But is that how we treat ourselves?" I shake my head. "We are far kinder to others than we are to ourselves. Really, self-love is flipping that script. It's not that you're always happy and in love with who you are. You're just kinder. You give yourself a break. You look in the mirror and say, 'It's okay, dude. I still love you.'"

I look across the bar. The woman in the "I Trust You" t-shirt is dancing as the waves beyond her do the same. "I meant to ask you," I say, clearing my throat. "Do you really look in the mirror each day and say 'I love you?' You talk about it in your book, but is it something you actually do?"

He nods. "Sure."

"Every day?"

Taking a deep breath, he stretches his neck from side to side. "I'm human. When things are going well, I tend to lose focus and miss a day. And then another. And another. We're not perfect, man. It's a daily practice, and sometimes you'll fall short. When you do, you have to start again. It's all about commitment. But you don't need me to tell you that the only way you achieve anything worthwhile is with commitment."

"True."

"There's no magical formula for loving yourself," he continues. "No 'Do this for sixty days and love yourself forever.' Each day, you have to wake up and do it again. Look in the mirror and say, 'I love you.' Some days, you won't believe it. Other days, you don't want to do it. But some days, you will. In time, it gets easier. But does it ever get easy? I doubt it. There are monks who spend a lifetime seeking inner peace, but at the end of it all, they're still human. They live. They feel. They die. You can make life easier by letting go of all that noise and not care what other people think.

You can make it easier still by being kinder to yourself. But life will continue to do its thing. Good, bad. It's what you make of it. I try to remind myself of that. Whatever happens, it's on me. I get to choose what I do and how I act. I don't get to control what happens, but what I do next is on me."

I run both hands through my hair. It's greasier than normal, much longer, too. I stretch my shoulders and straighten my back, feel the clicks and cracks. I spot the woman in the "I Trust You" t-shirt again, leaning over the bar and speaking to the guy manning it.

"I can tell you all this," Kamal continues, "but it doesn't matter. Nobody can tell you to let go. You're looking for permission, but there is none. You just have to take the leap and trust you'll figure it out."

I look at him, breathe, and feel a sense of relief washing over me. Like the waves out in front that crash into the beach, the water picks up silt and sand, transforms what is and makes it past tense. Over and over, for as long as time ticks. The same process is taking place inside me, present moments becoming part of the past, replaced by new ones that I get to choose.

NINETEEN.

Koh Rong, Cambodia

I love myself. I love myself. I. Love. Myself.

I whisper the words under hushed breaths, as though I'm fearful to let them out, let them be real. I keep trying to say the words in my head, to believe them, as Kamal suggested.

I read about his strange form of meditation in his book: look in the mirror and say the words out loud, look yourself in the eye and stare, to feel the words until you believe them.

I love you. I love you. I. Love. You.

"It works for me," he said. "But I don't know if it will work for you. You need to figure that out, find something that does."

I love you. I love you. I. Love. You.

Eyes closed, I slow my breathing and hang onto each breath. The fresh sea air flows in. The salt tingles against my throat and up my nose. It tickles but is pleasant. The sun begins its descent, the soothing heat warm against my face. The ocean is out there, beyond my eyelids.

I love myself. I love myself. I. Love. Myself.

My mind keeps wandering. I try to bring it back to those words, to believe them. I want to. I feel like I need to. But I'm not sure I do. Each time I say them, it feels like there's a voice deeper within saying, "No. No you don't. You can't."

I love you. I love you. I. Love. You.

Kamal had returned to our hut earlier, leaving me alone at the bar. "Just enjoy the sunset," he said. "Soak it in. Be with yourself."

I've stepped away from the bar and slumped into the sand mere meters away. I'm alone but barely. It's like I don't trust myself enough to venture too far down the beach. I'm on it, but only just.

I love you. I love you. I sigh. *I. Love. You.*

I allow the light in. It stings my eyes as I cup my hands and bring grains of sand to my nose, still warm as it slides through my fingertips, glistening in the fading light.

"Hey," says a voice. "It's a beautiful sunset this evening."

I arch my neck and watch her sit down beside me: the woman with the words "I Trust You" across her chest. "Hi," I say.

She says nothing, takes a deep breath, and runs her fingers through the sand. "I love this time of day." I look toward the horizon, a canvas of orange and blue. "I'm Gini, by the way."

"Ferdinand."

"I know. I saw you do a talk once. In New York."

"Oh."

She smiles. "It was good."

"Thanks."

"Is that why you're here? Speaking?"

"No," I say. "Taking some time away. Clearing the head."

"That's good. I imagine the life of a billionaire is pretty intense." I shrug. "If you want to be on your own—"

"No," I say. "Sorry. Just had a lot on my mind. Anyway, I'm not very good at it."

"At what? Being on your own?" I shrug again, this time with a smile. "I feel you. I didn't used to be, either. Always had to be around people."

"Not anymore?"

"Well, I'm definitely a people person, but I also love to spend time with myself."

"That's what I struggle with," I say.

"It can be hard. Especially if you're used to being around people all the time."

"Yeah. So, what's with the t-shirt? I noticed it earlier," I say, eager to change the subject.

She pinches each shoulder and pulls it back into position. "It's my way of showing people I trust them."

"Isn't that a little dangerous these days?"

"Why?"

"Because there are a lot of bad people. Especially for a woman in a country like this one."

"Yeah?" I nod. "How many have you met?" she asks.

"What do you mean?"

"How many rapists and murderers have you met?" she repeats.

I smile. "I can't say I have. At least, not that I know of."

She winks. "That's why I choose to trust people. I know there are bad people in the world, but I find it sad how our default setting is to not trust anyone. That they have to earn it before we let them in. Shouldn't it be the other way around?"

"I can't say I've ever thought about it like that."

"That's why I wear the t-shirt. To encourage you to." She places her hand on my thigh, looks me in the eye. "How does this make you feel?"

"Honestly?" I say. "A little tense."

"Why?"

"Because you have your hand on my leg. And you're staring at me. And we've only just met."

"Why's that a problem?"

"It's a little intense, don't you think?"

"Why?"

"I don't know. It just is."

She laughs, removes her hand, and glides it into the sand. "Touching someone is a sign of affection. And eye contact is a sign of trust and love. Why are they bad things?"

"They're not. I'm just not used to strangers coming up to me and invading my personal space."

"Exactly," she says. "Nobody is used to it anymore. We bump into someone on the street and say 'sorry.' We see someone who looks different from us and wonder what's wrong with them. We meet someone new, and instead of wondering what makes them beautiful, we look for signs of imperfection. There's no trust."

"I guess it's human nature to be wary of one another."

"Really?" She smiles again. "The ancient Greeks don't agree with that."

"Is that so?"

She nods. "The story goes that humans originally had four arms, four legs, and a single head made of two faces. We were powerful in this state. So much so that the gods felt threatened. They were worried we would overthrow them or not need them, so Zeus decided to punish us. He split us in half," she says, swiping her hand across her chest. "We were no longer whole, rather miserable, and we refused to eat or fight to survive. So Apollo decided to have us sewn back together but still no longer whole.

"Either male or female, not both. Two legs. Two arms. One face. We had our other half taken from us, and the story says that we've spent eternity since searching for the yin to our yang." She straightens her posture and looks out to the sea. "This is actually where the notion of having a 'soul mate' was born. Out there, somewhere, is our other half. Without knowing it, we yearn for them." She grabs my leg again, gently clasps it. "Deep down, everyone struggles to be on their own. It isn't natural. As a baby, you wanted someone around you. Each time they left the room, you felt abandoned. You worried they might never return. I'm not sure that fear ever fades."

I smile, take a deep breath, and hold it in my lungs. The sun is lower still, the orange darker, the black of the sky creeping in. "That's interesting. So for you, trusting others helps you trust yourself?"

"Trust is the foundation of everything," she says. "Happiness, growth, love—both for others and for yourself. It's much easier once you let your guard down and choose to trust."

"Self-love?" I ask.

"Mmm-hmm."

"Funny you say that. The guy I'm here with—"

"The one at the bar earlier?"

"Yeah. That's what we've been talking about: self-love. He wrote a book on it."

"Really?" I nod. "How serendipitous." She smiles, nudging my shoulder with hers. "I can only speak from my own experience, but once I chose to trust, I found loving myself easier. We spend so much of our lives wary of other people, blaming them for our own issues. But really, it's your problem. You don't trust yourself, so you project this mistrust onto others. They will hurt us, take from us, lie to us . . . We convince ourselves that the world is out to get us. We are the victims. Everyone else is to blame. We don't trust ourselves, so how can we possibly trust anyone else?"

"Maybe that's what love is," I say. "To trust someone else and let them in."

"Sure. But, again, it starts within. You can't love yourself unless you trust yourself."

"So do you?" I ask.

"Love myself?"

"Yeah," I say.

"I sure do." She smiles, wide and large. "I'm at the highest point I've ever been in terms of feeling comfortable in my own skin. I'm still growing and learning, but yes, today, I can honestly say I love myself. Maybe not always. But these days, I love spending time with myself."

"But you didn't used to, right?"

"Heck no. For most of my life, I've wanted to be on stage, seen by everyone. I wanted to be the center of attention. I measured how I felt about myself based on what other people said. I lived my life through their eyes. If they gave me approval, I felt great. If not, I didn't. I'd feel sad and angry and end up either blaming myself for being ugly or blaming them for being jerks."

I chuckle. "So what changed?"

"I don't know. I started to travel and meet people who inspired me. They were kind and genuine. They seemed to be happy and comfortable with who they were. They liked me for me. I didn't feel pressured to play a role, and I soon began to realize how much I relied on other people's opinions." She looks at me, sadness in her eyes. "I always thought I was a confident, independent woman, and that I was strong and didn't need other people. But I wasn't. It hurt, realizing this. I felt like a stranger."

"Yeah," I say, pursing my lips. "That's why I'm here, I guess. Trying to figure things out."

She grabs my hand. As soon as her skin touches mine, I feel a tense surge move up my arm. Anxious, I want to pull away. My heartbeat elevates. I feel it. I'm conscious of it. I want to avoid it. I don't know why. I'm safe. This is okay. There is nothing wrong with this. Yet every fiber of my being tries to convince me otherwise.

"I made a choice," she says. "We get to choose. If we don't like something about ourselves, we can choose to change or grow. That's what I did." She looks back out toward the sea, the sky growing dark. "I'll show you the video later, if you like, but basically, I went to New York City, stripped down to my underwear, put on a blindfold, and held a sign that read, 'I am standing for anyone who has struggled with a self-esteem issue like me. All bodies are beautiful. To support self-acceptance, draw on me.'"

"Wait, really?" She nods. "Why?"

"I wanted to step outside my comfort zone and do something that terrified me. The thought of strangers touching me, not knowing what they would write or do . . . that's scary."

"I bet."

"But I chose to trust them," she continues. "The thing is, to do that, I had to first trust myself."

"That's brave," I say. "I'm not sure I could do that. I'm struggling with you holding my hand."

"That's why you should." She looks at me again, holds her stare for a second. "That day unlocked something for me. I did it because I felt insecure about my appearance and saw it as an opportunity to face that fear. But while I stood there, near naked and blindfolded, I found myself diving into myself—past memories, fears I didn't even know I had—gaining a strange sense of peace from it all. Ever since that day, I've been on a journey to go deeper."

"Yeah?"

"Yep. That day only marked the beginning."

"So was this when you created the t-shirt?" I ask, pointing to it.

She nods. "I created one for me, initially. But the more people I spoke to, the more I realized how big a problem trust had become. So we started to run events and built an online community, and it's a full-blown movement these days."

"Really?"

"Sure. It's why I'm here. We're planning our next *I Trust You* retreat."

"That's cool."

"Thanks. I think so." She stretches her back and shoulders, cracks releasing as she does. "It's funny to think how it all began with a t-shirt. But it seems to give people permission to let their guard down and trust one another. Refusing to is so . . . exhausting," she sighs.

I think of Kamal, his advice to let go and let be. To be okay with who I am. To trust myself.

I love myself. I love myself. I. Love. Myself.

"I have an idea," she says, rising to her feet and pushing down on my shoulders. "But you have to trust me."

I look up, her face a silhouette as the sun shines a luscious orange behind her.

She holds out her hand. "Do you?"

"Do I what?"

"Do you trust me?"

"I'm not sure," I laugh. "It depends on what your idea is."

"Nope," she shakes her head and grabs my hand, encouraging me to my feet. "You must choose to trust me or not."

I take a deep breath.

I love myself. I love myself. I. Love. Myself.

TWENTY.

Canggu, Bali

I curl my toes in the sand, scrunching it into my skin. A small bird flies above, followed by another. I can't see it, but I hear the sea behind me. Waves climbing up and trickling over the beach's edge.

This time of day is calm, pond-like. The sky is darker, but not quite dark. The sun is still out, but nowhere near bright. Bali reaches out in front of me, an infinite ocean behind. I sip on juice, so fresh and delicious. No alcohol, despite Gini, Christian, and Wil all drinking. I didn't want to, so I didn't. My choice. I'm here because I chose to come. Gini asked me, and I said yes. I chose to trust her, to trust *this*. To let go, and let what will be, be.

She has a reason to be here. She's attending her friend's event. I have no reason to be here. But I have no reason to be anywhere. I suppose this is the point of this entire journey. To be open to what comes next, despite the lack of clarity around where it will take me. I feel the tension in my shoulders just thinking about it, my stomach seeming to resist it with an onrush of nausea.

You want control, it seems to tell me. *You need control!*

I'm not sure I've had control over anything for some time now. Not within me, that is for sure, but not inside of Contollo either. I spoke to Ray yesterday, for the first time since this trip began. He was fine. Everyone was fine. The whole company is fine. With me, without me—it doesn't seem to matter.

"Are you getting what you need from this sabbatical of yours?" he asked.

"I don't know," I said. "I'm realizing a lot about myself but no answers yet."

He sighed. I could practically see him shake his head and roll his eyes. "Well, you need answers soon. Plans are taking shape, and they will happen with or without you."

He hung up shortly after, rushing to get to his next meeting. I've always seen Ray as a mentor, a more experienced man there to help me along my way. Me, the captain, and he, my second-mate. The truth is, it's the other way around, and it has been for some time.

A few days have passed since I first met Gini on the beach; they've been slow and easygoing. I find this hard, too—the lack of things to do. The steadiness of nothingness. The time to think. Too much time to just . . . think.

I called Wil shortly after we arrived. "I did something I think you'll be proud of," I said. "I'm in Bali. In the last week, I've been to Spain and Cambodia. There's no reason for me to be here, other than I can."

"M'boy, that's great news. Such a beautiful country. Where are you?"

"Canggu."

"I'll be there in the morning," he had said, hanging up before I had a chance to question it. I thought about calling him back but decided not to. If he chose to come, that would be his choice. If not, that's fine, too. I'm here because I want to be, the same reason Kamal remains in Cambodia.

"I'm good," he'd said when I invited him to follow.

"You sure?"

He nodded. "I have some writing to do. This is a good place to do it."

His choice. That's okay. It's enough.

I felt anxious leaving him. I'm not sure why. I've known him less than a week, but I felt safe around him. At first, I struggled with our quiet and lackadaisical conversations. I wanted answers. I wanted action. I wanted to do something. He seemed so at peace with the emptiness and silence. I realized how uncomfortable I felt in it, afraid of it even. How fast paced I've allowed my life to become. Never time to reflect. No time to think or dwell or question. By design, maybe.

Kamal forced stillness upon me. I had no choice but to give in and drift within it, sitting on my thoughts. It isn't so bad. Peaceful, in fact. The thought of loving myself is maybe not impossible. Yet I still feel something holding me back. My chest remains tight. Something is going on in there. At night, I struggle to sleep. I just lay there, my mind jumping from one thought to the next. An inner voice tries to tell me something, but what, I do not know. Still, I'm noticing this voice. I'm conscious of it. I sense it's been there all along, but I've pushed it down and drowned it out. *The fact I'm hearing it now has to be progress, right?*

"What says you, Ferdinand?" asks Wil, snapping his fingers, and with it, my attention.

We're seated among scattered chairs and a small table, still on the beach yet inside the bar area. "About what?" I ask.

"Well, Gini, here, says that loving others is as important as loving yourself. Maybe more so. But me, m'boy? I don't think anyone needs anyone, so long as they trust in themselves. Which side of the line do you tread?" He smiles, glancing between Gini and me.

"I guess if you asked me a few months ago, I would say not," I say. "But these days, I'm not so sure."

"What have you done to my brother, Gini-girl?" Wil coughs, pushing his hands through his hair. "An untamed and untamable lion Ferdinand is. But here he is, practically stepping into a cage."

"I'm not exactly on the verge of marriage."

"M'boy, once the journey begins, it's already at an end." He shakes his head.

Gini wraps her arm around him, raising her glass with the other. "We're social animals, Wil. Even if you love yourself, it will never be enough. Why else do we have an oxytocin release when we're around someone we love? Why do we have an instant attraction toward some people? Why do certain people just make us feel safe?"

Wil laughs. "Because, as all animals are, we are horny."

"Where did you find this guy?" Gini asks me, shaking her head but smiling wide.

"Long story."

"Well, Wil, if you find yourself avoiding love for someone else, I'd say it's a sign to question what you're scared of."

"Sure. Sure. But who do you love, Gini?" Wil asks, placing his arm around her. "Other than me, of course."

She laughs, closing her eyes and arching her head back. "Seriously, where did you find this guy?"

"Don't ask," I say, sipping from the ice-cold fruit concoction.

"Well," Christian says, clearing his throat. "I need another drink. Shall I get a round in?"

I nod, as does Wil. Gini stands and moves toward him. "No, first you need to dance with me. You owe me one, remember?"

"That I can do," Christian says, looping his arm around hers and walking off.

"She's a good woman, that Gini," Wil says, watching them both move into the bar's shadows. "Are the two of you . . ."

I shake my head. "That's not what this trip is about."

"Ah, so you do have your eyes closed to it. Good boy."

"Honestly, I have no idea what I think about anything at the moment. But a woman would only complicate matters."

"Indeed, indeed," he says. "Resist that love, m'boy. No good comes from it. Although you don't need me to tell you that, as you know it all far too well." He peeks over his shoulder. "That being said, I may—"

"I figured you would." I laugh.

He sips from his drink, leans forward, and props his chin on his wrist. "I must say you seem different from when we last spoke."

"Yeah?"

"Oh, yes, oh yes. Less lost, although still wandering."

"I would say that sums it up."

"And that frustrates you?"

"What do you think?"

He shifts in his chair, aimlessly looking around the bar area. "Tell me, m'boy. Have you tried meditation yet?"

"In the past. Never liked it."

"Why is that?"

"Didn't work."

"And what did you expect it to do?"

"I don't know. De-stress and relax, clear the mind. That's the purpose of it, right?" He shrugs. "Do you?" I ask.

"Oh, yes. Almost every day." He places his hands in both pockets, shifts in his seat once more.

"I'm sure I've had a conversation with you before about how you hate it and those who do it." I say playfully.

He smiles, a wild grin. "Ah, yes, I've contradicted myself a lot over the last few years. But I find we all do. We only know what we know. What is true to us today will likely be disproved at some point in the future. After all, you can only be so stubborn for so long."

"So you find it helps?"

"Oh, yes." He holds a coin between two fingers, twirling it slowly.

"How?"

He pinches the coin between thumb and finger, holding it up. It's the same one he had in Dayton, the one with a carved triangle cut out of its middle. "Life is so fast," he says, pursing his lips. "If we don't force ourselves to stop, it passes us by with nothing but the middle finger to offer. But if you want to grow and get to where you want to go, surely you need to appreciate where you are right now."

"I think that's what I've realized recently," I reply. "These last few years, I've kept going and going. I guess I thought that's how you had to be. That if you stop, someone will come along and take it from you."

"And who would that someone be?"

"Who knows? That's the problem. You don't stop to think about any of it. You just react and get on with things and do what you think you have to, never stopping to ask what it is you want, what you need to do."

"Exactly." He points his finger at me. "You're beginning to see, to open your eyes. This is why you are different from the last time we spoke. Back then, you had your eyes closed. Didn't want to open them. But now, I see them peeking at me, m'boy." I smile and look down at the sand. "It's amazing what we see once we open our eyes," he continues, twirling the coin. "I used to have them closed, as you know. Most people out there in the world do. Walking blind, under a spell. No idea that they are."

"Was it meditation that opened your eyes?"

"Oh, no. I had to open them before I could become open to the idea of meditation. Like you, I tried it but didn't like it. I expected it to give me something, but it didn't. In fact," he says, looking around the beach, "I remember being here in Bali, meditating on some picturesque beach like this a few years back because that's what everyone I met did. I figured I was cool doing it, but the whole while, I thought the whole thing was stupid. It seemed to work for them, but not for me. So I began to make fun of people like that." He grabs his drink. "You know, m'boy. We've had conversations in the past, sipping expensive cocktails in pretentious bars. Making fun of people who likely made fun of us. Yet here we are, on a beach, saying that maybe they are right. But here's the tricky part," he continues, leaning close. "They aren't right. It's not about them being right or us being right. None of that matters. Right. Wrong. Any of it. But with your eyes closed, it's all you care about."

"So, what is the point?"

He smiles and takes a deep breath. "You ready?" I nod. "There is none." I roll my eyes and lean back in my chair. "It's true, m'boy. Once I let go of wanting to get something out of meditation or yoga or trying this or that, I started to get it. Once you let go, you get what you need. I don't meditate in the hope of getting anything from it. I do it because it gives me time to focus on me, be in the moment. Some days, I figure something out. Other days, I fall asleep. This morning, I lasted a few minutes before I needed the toilet. I don't care. I have no expectation."

I picture Kamal, his outlook on the outcome.

"I look after my body and eat better today—and drink less, most of the time—because I deserve it. Not because I want to look like an Adonis, but because I deserve better than a body filled with unnatural chaos. I don't do anything in the hope of getting anything anymore. The more you want something, the less likely you are to find it."

I sigh. "Yeah."

"Maybe that is why you remain frustrated, m'boy."

"Maybe. I see how uptight I've been, how I've been so focused on getting an answer. I know I have to let go of it, but—"

"It's hard."

"Exactly. Didn't you find it hard?"

He laughs. "Indeed. I found it mighty hard."

"So what did you do? What changed?"

"Meeting my main man, Turndog, helped."

"Of course. The man you cannot talk about."

He smiles, looking out to the horizon. "It's not that I cannot talk about him," he says. "It's that there's no point before you're ready."

"So I'm still not ready?"

He rubs his chin and bites his lower lip. "No. But I will give you what he gave me, before I was ready."

"Go on."

"His community is called [eso reo]. Does your phone have a signal?" I nod. "Type in esoreo.com. What do you see?"

I tap the words into the browser and wait for the page to load. Bit by bit, it appears. "Not much. It seems to be password protected."

"Is there a clue?"

"Yeah. It says, 'To enter this site, you must literally climb beyond the summit.' I don't get it. What's that supposed to mean?"

"When you figure it out, you'll be ready to see what's on the other side."

I laugh and arch my neck. "Come on. Can't you just tell me?"

"Absolutely not, m'boy."

"You know, I could probably hack my way into this site."

"I'm sure you could. But I'm even more sure you won't."

"Why's that?"

"Because your eyes are open. And with fresh, awake eyes, you can finally climb up the mountainside." He winks. "So do you think Gini likes me?"

"Changing the subject?"

"Oh, yes. You know me well, of course. She's a curious one, I find. I'd like to learn more about her, wouldn't you?"

I shake my head. "It's not what I'm after right now." I think of Beckie and how her leaving unintentionally began this journey. I wonder what she would think of me now, if she could see me questioning the very life she had questioned for a long time.

"Interesting. Interesting," he says, playing with his little coin once more. "It's all rather interesting."

"What is?" I ask, forcing the image of her out of my mind.

"All of this. The fact that we're here, on a beach, sipping cocktails as the sun dies another death. Would you have guessed we would be here the last time we spoke? No, of course not. You cannot see it, but you can choose to accept—no, embrace—whatever comes next. You always know night will come. But what it will bring is a mystery. Rain, wind, clear skies . . . a new kiss or a night of tears as you reflect on what you've lost, or as the case may be, never found. It's interesting, this life we're a part of."

"I guess," I say, leaning back in my own chair, knowing I've lost him to his own wandering mind.

"Here are my boys," a familiar voice says, appearing from behind a group of silhouetted bodies. "Hollis, this is Wil," Gini practically shouts, placing her hand on his shoulder. "And this is Ferdinand," she continues, pointing to me.

"Nice to meet you," the new stranger says, his face covered by a beard and baseball cap pulled down low. "You mind if I join you?"

"Sure," I say, motioning him to sit.

"I met Hollis a couple of years ago at some event, although neither of us can remember what it was," Gini says, sliding Wil over and sharing his seat.

Christian makes his way over with a tray of drinks and a drunken smile. The sky is dark now, most of the day behind us. I hear the waves over my shoulder. The beach is aglow with lit torches and fairy lights hanging from the bar's roof. More people have spilled onto the sand, with more to come, I'm sure.

The pond-like time of day is replaced with music, drinks, and laughter.

TWENTY-ONE.

Canggu, Bali

I stand on the edge of land where it meets water and the vast unknown beyond the horizon. My toes and feet sink into the sand, a fresh wave covering them and pushing me deeper. As the wave washes back out, I see no toes, feet, or skin. Just fragments of shell in and between the dark brown grounds of crushed rock.

The water is cool and refreshing, rising up my bare legs and under my blue swim shorts.

A gentle wind whips sand and salt into my skin, covering hairs with a light dusting. Another wave laps toward me, climbing further up the beach than the last. Closing my eyes, I take in a deep breath of the freshest air I can imagine. Not just fresh from the sea but from a brand new day.

Behind me, the beach remains dark: night. Out in front, the sun peeks over the horizon, pale colors of blue, orange, and yellow: day. I smile, alone on this beach that was so busy a few hours ago. We didn't leave until long past midnight. I barely slept. I drifted off for an hour or two but woke up ready to rise.

I'm tired yet feel refreshed. The air, the view . . . the fact that I'm up and watching the sunrise for the sake of it again.

I feel alive.

Of course, it wasn't my idea to do this. Hollis had suggested it. "Have you woken up for a sunrise here yet?" he asked. I shook my head. He laughed, as if my failing to do so was absurd. "Meet me here at 5 a.m. You won't regret it."

Our party dropped, one by one, leaving Hollis and me alone by a makeshift campfire on the beach. We sipped warm beer from cans and exchanged a joint. "Been a while since I smoked," I said as it numbed my throat and set my mind free. He said nothing, just sat and stared at the dancing flames.

We spoke for hours, talking about mutual friends, business, and his well-traveled life. Here searching for the perfect location for his next retreat, he and his partner have hopped from island to island. I hadn't heard of The Baby Bathwater Experience before, but I've met just about every name he shared with me. I hung on his words as he told me about past events and his plans for the future, feeling confused yet curious as he described why people attend.

"It's for business, but it has nothing to do with business," he said. "We just create unique experiences for entrepreneurs, so they can step out of their costume and unplug from the day-to-day. It's amazing what happens when you give people a chance to escape their realities." He sipped from his can. "I sense you know what I mean . . . since you left your own reality behind."

I opened up to him, sharing my story and recent journey and, for the first time, with excitement rather than frustration.

"The journey is the fun part," he said, folding a beer mat in half. "It's amazing how often we forget that when we have a big goal out in front. We obsess over it but then reach it and feel nothing," he continued, flicking the mat from his fingers. "You need to find something that lights a fire inside you, brother. No business or amount of money will satisfy you otherwise. You'll just end up sabotaging what you have. And then one day, you'll wake up and think, 'Is this it?'"

"Yeah," I sighed. "I'm realizing that."

"Don't fight it," he said, leaning closer to me. "Once you find that special something that ignites that fire, everything changes. You no longer search for a work-life balance—which is complete nonsense and doesn't exist, by the way—because everything you do is real and with purpose.

"I mean, my early businesses were sexy and scalable. They made a lot of money, and I could have made so much more with them than what I do now. But I felt miserable because it had no purpose. Whereas, what I do today—just hanging out with awesome people and giving them a chance to untether from their chaotic lives—I love it. Plus, I genuinely think I help them a lot more now than I ever could with a piece of software. No offense."

"None taken," I said. "And in the beginning, it wasn't about the software. It went way beyond a bunch of features and tech."

"But now?"

"Yeah . . ."

"I dig. It happens. It's easy to lose sight of what matters. There are a lot of distractions, you know?" he asked.

"I do. I'm coming to terms with the idea of change, but I can't get past how big the change will be. Whatever I do, I can't see how I'll escape blowing up my life. I mean, how do I let go of everything I've built? The thought of taking that leap, whatever it is, I don't know, I'm struggling with the whole idea of it."

"It's scary, dude."

"How did you do it? Walk away from your company like you did."

"I don't know. I just did. I didn't know what I wanted to do, but I knew what I didn't want to do. So I said 'screw it,' took that leap, and figured I'd grow some wings on the way down. It's scary, sure, but I love it. The leap is the best part. Don't you remember what it was like when you took it? When it was all new and nobody believed in you? When you had no idea whether it would work or not?"

I nodded, thinking about AJ and Kamal, and how they, too, spoke fondly of the leap.

"Amazing, right?"

"Yeah. It was."

"And it will be the next time," he said. "I always like to say, 'don't be afraid to go out on a limb because that's where the fruit is.' Yet too many people find something that works and tether themselves to the trunk, expecting the fruit to come to them. It doesn't work like that, brother."

A fresh wave washes over me, snapping me back to the present. I'm ankle deep in the sand now. I crouch and place my hands in the water, stretching my fingers and rubbing them into one another.

"Not bad, huh?" Hollis asks, approaching from behind.

"Morning."

"Been here long?"

"Ten minutes or so." I run my hands through my hair, stretch my neck and shoulders. "It is beautiful."

"Told you."

"So is this how you start each morning?" I ask.

"Nah. I don't usually get up so early."

"Really? I figured you would have some killer morning routine."

He shakes his head. "I used to, but it never did anything for me. I think life needs balance. Sometimes, you need to get up early, eat clean, and live a simple life. Other times, you need to let go and be more reckless–smoke, drink, and party hard." He faces me, his eyes red and tired. "You need to mix things up. Keep it fresh."

"So you don't start your day with yoga or a kale smoothie?"

He laughs. "I hate kale." He kicks the approaching wave. "I do value my mornings, though. I never get up early and work, for instance. Never check email or anything like that. I like to spend those first few hours on me. I just see how it goes. Some days, I want to get up and watch the sunrise. Other days, I go for a run. And some days, I roll over and get some more sleep."

"Yeah?"

"Sure. I go through periods. You only get one life, and it's too short to live and die by some routine."

"That's refreshing to hear," I say, smiling.

"How come?"

"Because it seems like everyone I meet at the moment has some transformational secret to share with me. I find it all a little—"

"Overwhelming?"

"Yeah."

"I hear you," he says. "Everyone has an opinion. And it's always the right opinion."

"Exactly."

"Don't worry about any of that, man. Be open to things, sure. But don't feel pressured to do any one thing. Not that you need any more advice, but mine would be to try it all without committing to any of it. We're all unique, and we find help in different places. For some people, a strict routine helps. For me, it doesn't. Maybe it will for you. Maybe not. You won't know until you try and see what works. And even when you find something that does, it may only work for so long." He raises his arms above his head and stretches them. "Nothing feels good forever."

"That makes sense," I say.

He walks along the shore's edge, the water covering his feet and ankles. "It's amazing what happens when you cut out as much external stimuli as possible: email, social media, news, reading, people and their dumb opinions . . ." He looks at me and smiles. "Mine included. You'll never figure out what you need if you try to listen to everyone else. Just spend a little time with yourself, dude. Learn to feel okay with who you are. There's no right or wrong in any of it."

"I know. I just find it frustrating, is all. I feel like I've already wasted a lot of time—"

"How have you wasted your time?" He cuts me off. "Doing what?"

"Like we talked about last night, chasing money and doing what everyone else wanted me to do. I feel like I've spent the last few years walking in the wrong direction."

"So you want someone to point you the right way?"

"That would be great." I smile.

"Dude, come on. Do you really need me to tell you that's dumb?"

"No," I say, sighing.

"It's like I told you yesterday, about the leap. It's the best bit," he says. "Scary as hell must be, and you never know what will happen from it, but you never will until you jump. What's the worst that could happen?"

"Oh, I don't know. I walk away from a hundred-billion-dollar business."

"So what?" I laugh. "I'm serious. So what? Let's say you did. Let's say you make some crazy decisions, like giving it away and donating all your money to charity. At the end of it, you're left with nothing. Would that really be so bad?"

"Well, it wouldn't be great."

"Why?"

"I'd have to start again."

"That's a bad thing? Come on, dude. You're as smart as they come. You'd make money doing something else, and you would likely find something even better. Deep down, you know that."

"Maybe I think that. But I don't know it," I say, firmly.

He smiles, wrapping his arm around both of my shoulders. "You gotta let go of the trunk, brother. You'll never get the fruit until you do."

I grimace a little and look down at my sand-covered feet.

He shakes his head, stops, and roots in his pocket for something. "It isn't real," he says, holding a few crumpled up dollars in one hand and a lighter in the other. It sparks to life, and he holds it next to the money. "I love money. I like what money allows me to do. The other day, I jumped out of a helicopter, and before that, I hired a boat so I could scuba. You need money for all that stuff. It serves a purpose. But it isn't *the* purpose." The notes alight, tiny flames dancing from the top of them. "Money is what you decide it to be. This stuff is just paper. I can spend it. I can set it on fire. I could give it all away. Whatever I do with it, I'm still me. It doesn't define me as a person. But by the sound of things, you allow money to define you. Whether it's wanting more of it or fearing losing it . . . it's got you."

He drops the flaming notes to the dry sand, a small but growing fire, gaining life, that will soon disappear and leave nothing but ash. He kneels and pokes a stick into the flames. "But I do get it. It's easier for a guy like me. I don't envy someone like you, with all that fame and responsibility. You don't get to be human. I get to do what I want, and it doesn't affect anyone. Most of the time, nobody knows what I do. Nobody cares. There aren't any eyes on me, but you?" He puffs out his cheeks. "People expect so much from you. I can't imagine what that pressure is like." He shakes his head and sighs. "Is it any wonder you've kept everything inside you these last few years?" He stands up, placing a firm hand on my shoulder. "You're doing okay, brother. What you're doing and the fact that you don't have all the answers you want . . . it's okay. You're okay. You're human, like the rest of us. Screw all those people who expect the world from you."

My eyes tingle. My chest is heavy. His words are made of metal, pounding into me like bullets. I want to fight them, fight back, and fight the emotions yearning to break free, like I always have. Push the inner voice below and drown it out once more. Rage against everything inside me that wants to step forward and be heard.

Yet instead, I fight that feeling, the resistance, and the fear.

I close my eyes, allowing tiny droplets to form in each corner. They drip from me and escape into the chilled morning air.

TWENTY-TWO.

Canggu, Bali

The backs of my legs throb as I attempt to touch my toes. My hamstrings prickle all the way up to my lower back, as if someone is carving them. I've never been flexible, but I didn't realize quite how inflexible I've become.

In an instant, I feel aged. No longer a young kid who can run and jump and play. I've always been lucky when it comes to my body. Naturally slim, there's never been a point where I've put on weight. In recent years, I've hit the gym regularly, and even on this trip, I drop for push-ups and sit-ups on the daily. But now, sitting in the sand as it grates against my thighs, I grit my teeth.

"You okay?" Jules asks, looking up as her chin touches her toes. I nod, barely. "Nearly done. Just a little cool down."

I nod again, releasing a whimper.

I've tried yoga once or twice before but never really understood the point of it. When I work out, I like to work out—a habit from my football days, I suppose, when coaches would ruin my body with preseason two-a-days. I hated it and loved it all the same—a challenge, and an end result that made me feel accomplished.

Instant gratification, like so much I've pushed for.

This is far from easy. We've only done twenty minutes, but I ache all over. I grit my teeth harder and push down on my legs a little further, edging ever so slightly closer to my toes though still far from touching them.

I met Jules for the first time last night, fresh from her women-only brainstorm with Gini. Along with Christian and Wil, the five of us had dinner, sharing drinks and stories. The last few days have passed quickly, hanging out and adventuring. Hollis took us to his favorite scuba spot. Wil insisted we visit a secluded beach he once went to. We've gone inland and along the coast, doing nothing but experiencing everything.

I've had more time to think, to just sit with my thoughts and appreciate the silence. It's been peaceful, but in some ways, it hasn't. I feel sad. I have laughed and smiled more in recent days than at any point on this trip, but a deep ache rests inside me, a sadness. It feels heavy.

I keep thinking of it: the pressure. The pressure I had no idea I was under until Hollis said, "You don't get to be human."

Those words, as simple as they are, hit me harder than any ever have.

I lay awake last night as everyone else slept, looked up at the starry sky, and letting myself feel: the pressure, the responsibility, the relentless need to be perfect, the role I have to play, the person everyone wants me to be, or at least, the feeling that I need to be that person. I realized I place as much pressure on myself.

Tears dripped down my cheeks as I silently wept. I've kept them at bay all these years in a bid to be the visionary and leader

I felt I had to be: the smartest person in the room, no matter the room I walked into.

A part of me sank, broken, drifting to the bottom of my inner ocean—a wreck, joining the other ships I've sunk over the years. The boy who loved to read, split in two. The young man who played football because he loved the game, torn to pieces. The little kid who dreamed such big dreams and didn't care about the outcome, blasted into tiny bits.

All sunk, scattered across the seabed, out of reach from light and life.

I came on this trip to figure out what to do next with Contollo. I know now that isn't the reason for all this. It isn't the company I've built, but the man I've allowed to build it. The busy man. The powerful man. The man with ego and self-importance. The man too important for this or them. The man who pushed away those who loved him, Beckie, and the rest before her, my parents, too, whom I barely speak to or see anymore.

The man who took the place of who I once was. As AJ suggested at the beginning of all this, maybe it's about me rediscovering who I am rather than becoming someone new.

I had the same dream again last night. It's the first time I've had it since this journey began. The same dream. The same details. The same panic and dread as I searched for someone I had lost. The same blurry silhouette just out of reach. The same crumbling rock as I pushed my fingers into it. Yet this time, as I fell, I didn't awake panting for breath. I seemed to float rather than fall, waking up calm to the fact. I just opened my eyes, aware of the dream and aware that I was then awake. Sweaty and lying on soaked sheets as normal but not panicked or shaken to the core.

A heavy feeling in my stomach is all I noticed, and the same heaviness remains now as I cling to my tingling legs and pull toward my toes.

"That's it," Jules says, pushing up on her arms and dropping into a cross-legged position. "How do you feel?"

I groan, pulling one leg up after the other. "Rough," I say. "I didn't realize how inflexible I am."

"Yeah, I think yoga may help you," she says with a smile, pushing her long brown hair away from her face.

"How long have you done yoga for?"

"Maybe six or seven years."

"Hope for me yet then."

"Yep. It's all about practice. I try and do a little every day, but I take it as it comes. I always find myself doing it more when I'm in a place like this," she says, pointing toward the ocean. "There's nothing better than doing yoga with this as your backdrop."

"It is beautiful."

She leans back and props herself up with folded arms. "So why did you want to join me this morning?"

"Trying to keep an open mind," I say. "Hollis told me how he has a 'grab bag' of things he likes to do each morning—doesn't have a routine but always takes something from his 'grab bag'."

"Grab bag . . . I like that. And you're thinking of putting yoga into yours?"

"Maybe. Figured I would give it a go."

She smiles, leans back into the sand a little further. "Sounds like you're questioning a lot of your life at the moment."

"You could say that." I laugh.

"It's good. Most people never do."

"It's hard, though."

"Yeah," she chuckles. "It is. But I think it's important that you do."

"Did you?"

"What, question things?"

"Yeah. But not just some things. It feels like I'm questioning everything. Everything I ever thought to be true. You know?"

"I know that feeling," she says, building mounds of sand with her hands. "We're all made up of our pasts. We believe so many things based on what we were taught or experienced. We grow up yet continue to live by these rules. If you don't question it—"

"Question what, exactly?" I interrupt, picturing Matt and our conversation back in New York, recalling how frustrated I felt back then, his words so vague and incomplete.

"Everything," she says. "What you know and don't know, how you feel and why." She pushes herself upright and faces me. Her brown eyes suit this early morning light, as does her tanned skin from months of venturing around one tropical paradise after another. Faint freckles litter each side of her nose, as though someone gently blew fine dust into her face. "We're all human," she says, "made of the same things: mind, body, spirit," she continues, pointing to her head, shoulders, and chest. "There are so many layers to each, all with questions and answers. Most people push them down, avoid them. Because it's scary and hard and, as I imagine you're finding at the moment, confusing . . . frustrating."

I smile. Nod. Breathe, in a bid to melt away the frustration I feel.

"Once you start asking a few questions, it's a Pandora's box. One question leads to another, and on and on and on. Forever."

"Forever, huh?"

"I think so. I certainly haven't got it all figured out yet." I feel the heaviness within, wonder if it will be with me forever. "It isn't always as confusing," she continues. "Most people start with the *mind*; they want answers but have no idea where to turn. So they read books and take courses and try and find someone to teach them, to give them the answers they crave. And these questions help. They open your eyes and help you wake up, but they don't really give you any answers.

"At some point, you have to put thoughts into action. I sense that's what you're doing now, trying new things like yoga. You're starting to focus on the *body*. You take what you learn and put it to work: your diet, your habits, and your routines. The mind and body work hand in hand like that. One fuels the other, and in a way it feels great, because you get some results. The problem is, all this really does is create more questions. You feel like there's something more you need, but you have no idea what it is. So you get more frustrated, and I think that's why most people end up quitting and saying things like, 'It didn't work for me.'"

"You mean, like how a lot of people start yoga but then quit after a few weeks?"

"Exactly. Let's take dieting, which is something everyone tries at some point. They decide they need to change and lose some weight. So they read some books and articles . . . *mind*. They then put this to the test and start a new diet, maybe even hit the gym and hire a personal trainer . . . *body*. At first, it's great. They lose weight. They feel good. They're healthier. But at some point, they will likely lose focus and go back to bad habits. Or worse, they actually achieve what they wanted, but they still don't feel satisfied. So they try something new . . . read a different book or take a different course or commit to the latest diet. Why do you think that is?"

"I don't know. It's hard to change, I guess."

"It is. But it's harder when you don't understand why you need to make the change in the first place. Where the real problem comes from. The root cause."

"What do you mean?"

"Why you were overweight to begin with. Maybe it's a genetic issue. Maybe you ate to block out some form of pain. Maybe you felt stressed and turned to food. By working on your mind and body, you can fix a lot of your problems. But it doesn't help you figure out who you are or, more importantly, why you are."

"The *spirit*," I say, more to myself than to her.

"Yes. I'm not talking religion or spirituality here either. It is that for some people, and that's fine. But it's more to do with that inner compass that lives inside of you and tries to guide you," she says, pointing at my chest. "It's what you cannot see or make sense of, but you feel it's there." I look at her finger, feeling the heavy ache on the other side of it. "Once you start to focus on those questions—which is hard, because they suck—that's when you begin to make real progress. You start to let go of the frustration and replace it with acceptance. There are still questions. There's still progress to make and things to figure out. But you start to get to the root cause."

"That makes sense," I say. "These last few days, I've started to become aware of something. I don't even know how to describe it—something inside me, trying to tell me something."

"Your compass," she says, smiling, her crisp white teeth on show. "Whether you start with your mind, body, or both, it pushes you down a rabbit hole. Your eyes begin to open, and you realize how noisy you've let your life become. So you quiet it down and begin to hear that voice, that compass." She takes a deep breath, slowly letting it back out. "We all want to drive the ship, but we can't. Our *spirit* does. Once we let go of the wheel and allow it, that's when the magic happens."

"Magic, huh?"

"Yeah. At least, it feels like it. Opportunities appear and luck seems to find you. It's as though something inside you clicks, and it welcomes the universe in as you go from confused to enlightened."

"And you went through that?"

"Absolutely," she says, twirling a chunk of her long dark hair into tight curls, layers of various brown hues catching the light.

I hang on her words as she dives into her tale of slipping into debt after her business partner—and then boyfriend—embezzled money out of her business. For eight months, she worked harder and longer than ever before to keep her head above water. I look into her eyes as she relives the pain. She blinks, slowly, seeming to remember the feeling of each doubt and worry, the panic, and the attacks.

"It was a tough period," she says. "I hit my limit and knew I couldn't continue. It wasn't the life I wanted, and I knew something had to change. So I stopped everything. I literally shut down my business and told my clients I would be away for a while. I asked my father for a loan." She shakes her head. "I hated that. I felt like such a failure. But he supported me, and it gave me some time to figure things out."

"You went on your own sabbatical?"

"In a way. But not like you are. Instead, I decided I would say no to everything for sixty days."

"Really?"

"I know, weird, right? Everyone always says you should say yes, but I felt like that is what I had always done. I kept saying yes to everything and everyone, afraid if I said no, I'd lose out. So for sixty days, I decided I would say no. Each business opportunity. Each request. Each idea. The answer to all of it was . . . no." She laughs. "I found it so hard at first—totally out of my comfort zone. But after a few weeks, I began to hear myself . . ." she trails off. "That inner voice that begged me to listen for so long, suddenly I heard it. It was amazing. For the first time in my life, I started to realize what a real yes looked like."

"A real yes?"

She takes another deep breath and smiles, her eyes squinting as she does. "Most of us say yes to things we think we need to say yes to, but in reality are just *maybes*. I realized how often I said yes to a maybe: a five-out-of-ten." She shakes her head again. "Life's too short for that, don't you think?"

"Yeah," I reply, rubbing my chin, thinking about my own inner voice of late and what it's trying to tell me.

"I decided the only things worth saying yes to are the ten-out-of-ten, heck yeses that you don't have to think about. And guess what happened?"

"More heck yeses came your way?"

She nods. "It's like I trained my environment to align with what I truly wanted, what I needed. I kept meeting amazing people, and one opportunity would come after another. All that worry and stress from before . . . gone." She swipes her hand over the sand. "In fact, it's how my business, The Unconventional Life, began—because I got invited to write a column for a magazine. It didn't feel like a heck yeah, so I proposed a podcast instead. The old me wouldn't have done that. I would just have said yes and written some bland column for a few weeks."

"And they said yes to the podcast?"

"They loved the idea. It built traction straight away. Without the podcast, I wouldn't have started the events that are my mission today and wouldn't be living a life where I get to do what I want, when I want. I would probably still be hustling and grinding just to get by."

"All because you said no," I say again, more to myself than her.

"No," she says, cupping my hands in hers. "Because I started to say yes."

I nod and look at her eyes as they stare into mine. Rich and dark brown, like two cups of coffee. So different than mine, which are light and blue. It seems I should feel uncomfortable, holding her hands with her staring like this. I don't. I feel calm and warm inside—at peace.

She pushes up and springs to her feet with little effort, towering over me and peering down. "None of it would have happened if I didn't dive within and go deep down that rabbit hole. The mind, the body, they're important. They matter. But only if they lead you to what's in your spirit and then only if you let go of the wheel and let it guide you."

She walks behind me and crouches, leaning on my shoulders. "Ferdinand," she says quietly into my ear. "I have no idea what you're searching for. I sense you don't know, either. That's okay. But as long as you avoid what's inside, you'll never find what you're looking for."

TWENTY-THREE.

Venice Beach, Los Angeles

Once more, I'm on a beach, standing with feet in dry sand as I look out to the setting sun. The ocean glistens. Palm trees to my right reach high into the sky. Volleyball nets to my left are vacant and empty. I've spent more time on the beach these last few weeks than in my whole life combined. I've never been a huge fan, as tiny grains work into uncomfortable places. Yet of late, I've found comfort here.

It's a different beach from those in Bali and Cambodia. But the setting is the same.

Sea, sun, sand, and waves. They lap against the shore before returning to the deep. The water that touched Bali will one day touch here, all part of the same system, a bigger picture than I can see. I've thought a lot in recent weeks about the aspects of life I cannot see. I've placed so much emphasis on the things I can, focused on what I could touch—money, how I look, how the women I sleep with look; places, people, the phone I hold or TV I own;

pictures I can take of the things I'm doing; follower, numbers, and media mentions, the number of zeros. I've distracted myself with the senses I own, losing any sense of what exists below—the aspects of life, of myself, that I cannot touch or see but can feel, if I allow myself to—love, trust, faith in myself and others, that inner voice and yearning, the pressure, the sense of peace.

I've overlooked it all and pushed it to one side, refused it a voice. No time for it. No need for it.

I keep thinking about my conversations with AJ, Matt, Ishita, Kamal, and Hollis. How I pushed for answers, hounded them with broad questions. I've been so desperate for a quick fix to a problem I don't understand, haven't taken the time to ask: *Why do I hurt?*

What is this feeling? Who is this person?

Maybe I'm afraid to fail or, worse, to succeed, truly succeed, truly have a lasting impact. Am I good enough or worthy of something like that? So many people already rely on me and expect so much from me.

My head spins all the time.

I feel greater peace than maybe I ever have, but the more time I spend on my own, the more sadness and emptiness I feel. I cannot settle on a thought. I ask a question, and it leads to many more. Like a badly scratched record, it skips from note to note. *What am I so afraid of? Why can't I quiet these thoughts? Why do I want answers to questions I don't dare ask? Where did all this come from? When did it all begin?*

In part, I feel enlightened. I've discovered so much about myself. But in truth, nothing at all. I'm as confused now as I have ever been, maybe more so. This journey, the people, the stories shared . . . they've brought no clarity. I've replaced blind bliss with mindless chatter.

Yet despite this, I feel calm.

Something seemed to click as I sat on the beach with Jules that day. Not an answer. But a question: *What's really going on?*

I realized something real was going on deeper inside me. I felt it. I have for a long time. In that moment, I gave myself permission to face it, to let it in, to let it be.

Jules continued to share stories and talk about her work with The Unconventional Life. I listened, but my mind kept wandering back to that question: *What's really going on?*

From the people she had interviewed on her podcast to those she's worked with at events, she kept coming back to that inner voice, the spirit that supposedly houses all those answers I'm so desperate for. She talked about her music and how she's found time to pursue it in recent years. Not because she has more time but because she decided it was important to her.

Faces appeared before me again: Kamal, Hollis, Ishita, AJ. . .

None of them were busy. None of them appeared strained by the life they lived. None of them had more money, fame, or power than me. Yet they all seemed to have much *more* than me.

"I played at Burning Man a few weeks ago," Jules said. "I opened for The Alan Parsons Project. A few years ago, I couldn't have imagined that."

"Burning Man?"

"Yeah. You been before?"

I shook my head. "Heard about it. Never really understood it."

She laughed. "There are no words to describe it, that's why. Burning Man is a place that cannot be compared."

"It's just a bunch of people taking drugs, right?"

Another laugh. "No." She grabbed my arm and pulled me down to the ground, the two of us cross-legged and facing the other. "There are a lot of drugs at Burning Man, but that isn't the point. The reason people go is to align with their flow."

"As in, 'get in your zone?'"

"Yeah. But in a conscious way. Everyone has found flow at some point, be it in their work or doing something they love. But do you know how to tap into it? Can you get into it whenever you want?" She opened my palms and rested her fingers on them. "In the real world, there's a lot of pressure to be someone. Everyone is out there living a life they feel they have to. And there's truth in it, too. You can't always do what you want, when you want. But at Burning Man, you can—within reason."

"No killing people, then?"

"No. No murder. But you can be who you want to be. You can, if you want, create a new identity. You can experiment and say yes to what you want to say yes to. There's no 'no.' It's a playground that allows you to play. Just like you used to as a child." She closed my palm and wrapped her fingers around mine. "Nobody expects anything from you. Everyone is there looking for the same thing. They just want to be open to whatever and commit to nothing. It's crazy and surreal, and if you go there with an open mind, you can literally find anything."

"Like what?" I asked.

"Anything. One minute, you may get invited to an orgy and, the next, take part in an impromptu dance party. Opportunities surround you the entire time, and it allows you to fulfill pretty much any fantasy or curiosity you have ever had. All the while, you're surrounded by people who are saying, 'It's okay. We won't judge you.' It's not about doing anything, but rather, having the opportunity to. It's freedom in its purest form. It gives you permission to let go of resistance. You say no when you want to and yes when you want to."

"Find those ten-out-of-ten yeses," I said to myself.

She squeezed my hands. "Yes. You let your guard down and come up with ideas like you never have before. Some of the best I've had came at a *burn*. You're surrounded by other people sharing them, crazy and surreal ones. You collaborate. You don't mean to. You're not consciously doing so. It just happens. It's amazing."

I looked at my hands, and I felt no discomfort; I didn't feel the need to remove them from hers. "Burning Man is a place where you don't always get what you want, but you find what you need," she said.

She continued with stories about people she met there and the various things she had seen. But she seemed to hold back, not letting me in completely. She kept saying, "You need to experience it yourself. Words alone will never come close to explaining it."

I've read about it since. *Flow* is a topic that keeps coming up. Hollis recommended I read a few books from a friend of his, Stephen Kotler. I read *The Rise of Superman* on the plane, cover to cover, as I flew across the Pacific and back to the States. It's filled with stories about how people find *flow* and, more importantly, keep it.

I've always known of *flow*, in the same way I've known about *mindset* and *love* and *trust*. But I haven't understood it. And still don't.

I keep thinking about who I used to be growing up. At school, when I played football and led the team as the quarterback, time seemed to cease. Entire quarters would fly by in seconds, but when it counted, the final two minutes could last forever. I locked in on the task at hand, seeing everything but thinking about nothing. That's the only way to play when the game is on the line. As the years passed, and the games played a more important role in what came next in life, I seemed to lose that. I was focused more on whether I was good enough to play in college, weighing up the game against the rest of life's responsibilities.

I played but not in that zone where time is malleable.

So I quit. I kept telling people that I'd fallen out of love with the game, replaced it with coding, which led me to Contollo. But I'm not sure I did fall out of love with it. Maybe I just got so distracted by all the pressure that I lost sight of what I loved most about it. Maybe that's what's happening now.

I'm distracted by all the noise from others, consumed by all the pressure, allowing myself to fall out of love or, at least, tricking myself into believing it. Maybe I still do love it. Maybe I just don't love what I've let it become.

A few days ago, I bought another book Kotler wrote, *Stealing Fire*. For the first time ever, I'm listening to a book as I walk each morning along the beach and through the streets of Venice. Each day, my alarm goes off at 6 a.m. When it does, I ask myself, '*Do I want to get up right now?*' Some mornings I have. Other mornings I've rolled over.

Whenever I do rise, the first thing I do is go for a walk. I listen to the audiobook as Kotler dives deeper into *flow* and the rabbit hole it continues to push me down. I walk with no purpose, other than to walk. Yesterday, I walked five miles. Today, just one.

A week's passed since I left Hollis, Jules, and Gini in Bali. Wil left a day before me, returning to Dayton for a meeting. As a group, we continued to laugh, drink, and enjoy life. We did a great deal of nothing, taking each day as it came. No plan. No schedule. I let the unstructured peace enter my life, no longer resisting it or that inner voice.

"I'm going back to America today," I told Christian the morning of my flight. "I've already booked my ticket."

He almost spat out his coffee. The two of us stood alone on our wooden hut's porch. "You booked a flight?"

"I did."

"I never thought I'd see the day." He smiled, sipping from his steaming cup. "When do we leave?"

"*We* don't," I said. He looked at me, said nothing, and seemed confused. "These last few days, I've felt a weird, heavy ache in my stomach," I explained. "I've loved it here. I can't remember the last time I felt so satisfied. This trip, so far . . ." I drifted off, unsure of what I wanted to say. "It's been strange. For most of it, I've felt frustrated. I still do. It's all confusing, but I've started to realize I'm looking to other people for answers and avoiding the exact place I need to look."

"Which is?" he asked.

I pointed to my chest. "Last night, after everyone went to bed, I stayed up and looked out at this," I said, motioning to the view of trees and fauna, the endless blue beyond. "It felt good. It's been a long time since I last felt good on my own. And it was in that moment I realized why you're here." I sipped from my coffee. "I'm scared." His eyes widened. "I was scared to come on my own. In fact, I've felt incapable of surviving on my own for years. I've tricked myself into thinking you are my assistant who allows me to do what a CEO needs to do. But in truth, you are my safety net. There, each day, so I have someone. I keep you close enough so I'm not alone but push you far enough away so you don't get to see what's going on inside me. I've done the same to all those women and everyone else in my life. Pushed them away but kept them just there, just close enough . . . just in case I needed them. I did it to Beckie. She loved me, and I kept saying that I loved her. But I didn't. I just needed her. I needed her there, next to me, just like I've needed you."

I looked away, rubbed my face with both hands. Felt the guilt. Let it consume me. Just let it be.

"I'm sorry, Christian. We were friends, once. But in recent years, I haven't allowed us to be. I've held you back." I paused, looked at him, saw him for the first time in so long: my friend. "I'm sorry."

I didn't intend to apologize. I didn't begin the conversation with any aim, other than to say I would continue the trip on my own. But the more I said, the more I had to say. I could see how uncomfortable the whole conversation made him. I imagine he, too, felt conflicted in recent years. I was his safety net as much as he was mine.

As the morning sun rose higher in the sky, I reassured him he didn't have to worry about work, that he could choose whatever role he wanted. I would support him however I could and in whichever way he would like. The more we spoke, the more excited he became. We talked about him, what he wanted. I asked him about his plans and dreams.

Memories flooded forward of past occasions when we worked late, went to dinner, and spoke about life, confiding in one another, laughing with each other. I recalled the moment he *came out* to me. It didn't surprise me, but I remember feeling pride. Pride for him but also for myself. He'd told me. He'd trusted me enough to let me in on a secret he'd kept inside for so long. Would he trust the person I'd become since? I doubted it.

"What's next for you?" I asked, as morning became noon.

"I'll stay here for a while," he said. "I may even travel. See some of the world."

I nodded, grasped his shoulder. "Good. It's time you did you."

We sipped coffee until the mood turned to something deeper. We talked. We've talked since, almost every day, in fact, as we share texts and pictures. No schedule. No, 'here's your to-do list.' Just friends talking as friends do. I'm here, alone, finally, after far too long. I look out to the ocean. No answer out there. I close my eyes, dive within. Still so many questions in there. I smile.

I love myself. I love myself. I. Love. Myself.

For once, I believe it.

TWENTY-FOUR.

Venice Beach, Los Angeles

It's almost dark now, the final remains of the sun clinging on for dear life.

The horizon glows. The ocean below it is a rich, navy blue, soon to be black. Clouds seem to dance above, mixing with the orange remnant of the day, soon to become night. I take a deep breath, pull in the cool, salty air. Keep it there. Smile. Let it out, now warmer from its trip.

I've spent the entire day alone. No phone calls or conversations with another human being, other than a couple of passing *pleasantries* when exchanging money for coffee. Ray tried to break the silence, calling four times during the afternoon. He left a voicemail after the third and sent a text after the last. He wants to talk. He wants to know when I'm coming back. I'm not sure if he's awaiting news from me, or if it will be the other way around. I have a sense, though it may be nothing but a story I've made up in my head, that life has gotten easier for those at the top since I left.

It makes sense to have someone older and more experienced take the reins as the company transitions into a new realm. Do they really trust me with a hundred-billion-dollar company? Would I trust me? Does someone like me even have a role to play in a company like that? Have I played a significant role these last few years or just masqueraded as someone who does? I imagine Ray misses me but more because he's worried about me rather than needing me back in the office. We've been through a lot together. He's seen me grow from boy to man, although I'm not sure if he's helped me become a good one.

I feel the need to push him away, to distance myself from him. In recent years, he's been the one person I haven't kept at arm's length. I confided in him and turned to him, but now I can't imagine being in the same room with him. It's strange, but even though I know I've pushed so many people away and kept them just out of reach, I feel compelled to do the same now—like some sort of bad habit I can't shake free of. I should call him or at least reply to his text. But I won't. I know I won't. Not tonight.

Maybe in the morning.

I laugh under my breath, shake my head, and puff out my cheeks. The same narrative as always goes on within, only now I'm conscious of it. It feels like I'm both part of the conversation and an onlooker, amused by the irony of contradictions and hypocrisy.

I'm a work in progress, I guess. I feel okay with that—calm, at ease, despite the whirlwind of thoughts and questions battling inside my mind. That heavy ache within is still there. But the chaos above isn't as painful as it once was. The pressure and worry and frustration replaced with a sense of indifference—that all will be okay because it will be okay. I am okay.

I am okay. I am okay. I. Am. Okay.

I smile. And feel the smile. It feels nice, genuine. Not forced. Not for show. Not because someone else has said or done something amusing. Just because I feel like I want to. A smile for the moment. I push up on my hands and twist on the wall until my back faces the dying sun. I look at those who pass me by, a rush of people walking in every direction. Three guys with long and messy hair stand in a circle, talking, each with a skateboard in hand. A family walks past with a young boy on his father's shoulders, surely up past his bedtime. A mother and daughter stroll beside them, hand-in-hand, with ice cream in the other. A girl on rollerblades skates by, wearing short shorts and a top not much bigger. A man on his phone strides past with no clue of what's going on around him.

A young couple lean against a pole, inches from each other's face and staring deep into each other's eyes, unblinking, lips at the ready. They kiss, lean their foreheads against one another. In this dying light, they come together to form a single silhouette.

They seem to be in *flow*, present in the moment and oblivious to the crowd around them.

Just the two of them, not caring about everyone else.

I'm not sure if I've ever had that with a woman. I think of Beckie and feel sad because I know she has looked at me like that, yet I have no memory of a time when I stared into her eyes with the same presence. To experience *flow* with another person, is it different from having it on your own? Each thought seems to come back to this: *flow*.

As I listen to Kotler talk about it in *Stealing Fire*, I keep pausing the audio to stop and think, trying to recall what it feels like, like a drunken memory that only tells part of the story. I've had it; I know I have. But what's it like? How does it feel? How can I have it again?

There's a section in *Becoming Superman* that I keep thinking of, too. It spoke of *mothers, musicians, and marshmallows*—how so many typical, successful people have at least one, often all three. The *mothers* represent a supportive upbringing, where parents and teachers guide you and are there for you, giving you what you need, showing up for you, and pushing you to be your best. The *musicians* represent those who have put in the hours, immersed themselves in a skill and locked in mastery—the notion that those who have put in ten thousand hours of conscious practice will always be better off than those who haven't. And then there are the *marshmallows*, those who represent an exercise I went through myself at four years of age—sat down, left in a room on my own, with a simple instruction to not eat the marshmallow. If I resisted, I would get two. Those who resist are set up for success later in life. They're able to delay gratitude. They're capable of looking beyond the moment and thinking, instead, of the bigger picture. To strategize. To plan. To climb the ladder while everyone else lives in the moment.

I didn't eat the marshmallow. I resisted. I sat on my hands and hummed a tune, thinking about the coming reward. I also had supportive parents, tutors, and coaches who laid the foundations for my excellence. By the time I arrived at Stanford, I had well over ten thousand hours of conscious, purposeful practice behind the screen, coding and hacking my way to mastery.

I had all three: *mothers, musicians, and marshmallows.*

I've only ever known success because of it. I was always destined for more, forever placed on a pedestal of impossibly high expectations. But this isn't the side of the story Kotler focuses on. He shares stories about misfits and rebels who had none of this yet still became masters of their world. The underlying reason seemed to reside in this notion of *flow*, and how there are two types of people, on extreme ends of a scale: *presents and futures.*

People in the *present* are hedonistic pleasure seekers who live for now and don't care about tomorrow. Whereas those who plan for the *future* are patient and ambitious go-getters who can see the path before them.

I'd never thought about it, but as I read the words on the page, they seemed to drift up and become one with my eyes. It's so obvious and so clear; even as a young kid, I obsessed about the future and would push all focus of *today* to one side. It worked, too. I won. I kept winning and growing and succeeding, gaining awards and accolades and a life that everyone seemed to envy.

He's so smart.

He's so talented.

He's destined for greatness.

Everything I did was coordinated and with purpose. I had to win. Not necessarily now, but later, when it counted, I'd come out on top.

Be a billionaire.

Be famous.

Be the best.

I shake the thoughts from my head and look at the young couple so present and in this moment; this very second, her head leaning on his chest, their arms around each other. They're living life right now, no need to think about tomorrow or the future down the line: *What if they break up? What if they stay together and get married? What will their kids be like? Who will be the breadwinner? Where will they live? If they remain together, does that mean neither of them will have sex with anyone else ever again? Will one of them cheat? Will this feeling they have for each other last?*

Will they regret taking a chance on one another in the future?

Will they get to the end of their lives and wonder, *what if?*

Lost in the future: my life summed up. It's great until it's not, and as the stories in *Becoming Superman* suggest, those who live that way become workaholics who burn out, push people away, see others as a burden, and always wish for more, even when they get everything they want. My face should be on its front cover.

I close my eyes.

I am okay. I am okay. I. Am. Okay.

I love myself. I love myself. I. Love. Myself.

I slow my breath, try to slow my mind with it. I can change. I can change the narrative if I choose to. Opening my eyes, I smile because I can. I feel it. I try to just be here, right now, share the moment with that couple, share it with all these people as they pass by, living their lives, some *present* and others in the *future*, all of us broken and searching for the pieces to fix who we are.

I love myself. I love myself. I. Love. Myself.

TWENTY-FIVE.

Kenneth Hahn State Recreation Area, Los Angeles

He sits back against a tree, eyes shut, a smile on his face as he breathes in, holds it, and releases it again. "It's very peaceful here," he says, opening his eyes. "Don't you find it amazing, the effect a little nature can have on you?"

I look around. We're surrounded by green grass. The occasional paved path splits sections in two, leading up to benches and makeshift barbeque areas. Trees dot the landscape, some taller than others, all green and lush, alive and thriving in the sunshine. I sit, too, my back straight and legs crossed. Sticks from the tree above and faded, fallen leaves prickle my legs. I nod. "It's a recent revelation of mine. But, yes, I agree."

"Jules said you were keen to meet more people who have been to Burning Man," he says. "You thinking of going next year?"

"I'm not sure. Maybe. It does seem cool. Crazy but in a good way, I guess."

"Oh, it's crazy. Unlike anything else in the world."

I've spoken to Jules a few times since we went our separate ways. She's currently in Morocco, scouting for her next event. When I mentioned that I was in Los Angeles, she said, "I think my friend Michael Sanders is there. The two of you should meet. He's just come back from Burning Man."

Within a few hours, we were exchanging texts and agreed to meet here in the park. I arrived early so I could roam among the trees and allow my mind to wander. Once more, I've spent most of the day alone. Just me and my thoughts, the thought of *flow* never far away.

I finished *Stealing Fire* this morning. In both of his books, Kotler suggests that it's *flow* that creates clarity and balance. For those in the *present,* it pulls them toward the future and gives them the ambition, motivation, and structure they're so often missing. For those of us stuck in the *future*, it brings us into the moment and allows us to enjoy it, treasure it, and be okay with who we are and where we are.

I realize I've never allowed myself to live in the present and be grateful for where I am and what I have. I've been too busy clinging to the past, desperate to avoid repeating its mistakes, and then dreaming of the future, desperate to have all the things I can and feel I should have. Because if I don't have them, what will I be? Will I be enough? What will all those other people think? I'm pushing and hustling and reaching for *it*, which is always out of reach, but I'm okay with that because it keeps me focused and driven. The next step is more important than this one. It's better. I'll be happier there. I'll have more, be more, maybe, finally, feel like I'm enough.

The heaviness within grows heavier by the day as I sit on these thoughts. It's who I am and who I've always been—ungrateful and unable to enjoy the people around me because I might meet better ones later.

"From what Jules tells me, it sounds like you've been on quite a journey," Michael says, his eyes locked on mine, bringing me back to the moment. Once again, my mind was elsewhere.

"You could say that," I say.

"How's it been?"

"Good, I think. Although I'm trying to figure out exactly what I've figured out."

His eyes remain on mine, unmoving and still. There's a kindness to his smile. Long, dark hair engulfs much of his face. The rest is covered with a thick beard. A nose and rosy cheeks the only parts untouched. I notice the slight wrinkles beneath his eyes, formed after a thousand smiles and countless laughter. They reach up toward his forehead, a unique pattern all his own, like a piece of paper pinched in each corner. Beads and bangles cover his wrists, and two necklaces hang from his neck. In his baggy shorts and tattered green vest, I can picture him in the desert. I've begun to form an image of the sort of person who goes to a *burn*. Michael fits the description. I'm not sure I do.

"Jules says you were just at Burning Man."

"I was."

"How was it?"

Without taking his light brown eyes off of mine, he pauses and seems to consider his words. He's slow, purposeful, and present. "Every burn is different," he eventually says. "But the feeling I have when I leave is always the same: refreshed. It's a place that refills your cup. It's like a reboot. I don't think it matters who you are—we all need that."

I place my arms behind me, lean back, and stretch my neck. "That's another recent revelation of mine." A dog barks in the distance. "You've been a few times, right?"

"I have."

"Is that why you keep going back? To reboot?"

"It's not the only reason. But it's one of them."

"Why else?" I press. "No one has anything but good things to say about it. And from what I've read and seen, it does look amazing. But—"

"But it's just a bunch of crazy hippies doing crazy stuff in the desert?"

I laugh. "Yeah."

"Whatever you are looking for, you'll find it at Burning Man. It's hard to describe what it's truly like because everyone gets something unique from it."

I roll my eyes. "That's what I hear."

"I know. It's a cliché everyone uses. Like when parents say you won't get it until you have a kid of your own."

I nod.

"It's true, though. I can sit here and share one story after another with you, but you won't *get* it until you experience it. Isn't that true with most things in life?"

"I guess." I feel a frustration within. Just notice it. "So, what's your story? Other than being a Burning Man veteran."

Another smile. Gentle once more. The creases around his eyes on show. "My current project is Horizon Blockchain Games."

"Games, as in video games?"

"Kinda. But it's a whole new dimension of gaming. It uses a blockchain infrastructure to bridge the gap between the digital and physical world, ensuring everything belongs to its players and creators."

"Interesting," I say. "I've been meaning to look into blockchain technology for a while now. I have a feeling it will impact how we communicate with each other. But I don't know. I need to explore it at some point."

"What's stopping you?"

I sigh. "Time, I guess. I never seem to have enough of it for new ideas like that."

"Until recently," he says, brushing his unkempt long hair out of his face. "These days, you have nothing but time, right?"

"I guess I do." I feel uneasy, conscious of the resistance. Contollo, work, the future of it all . . . each time I think about it, my chest aches and my head pounds. I shake the thought. "So you been involved in it for a while? Blockchain, I mean."

He nods. "For a few years. I find it fascinating, and the potential it has is unrivaled. The moment I first heard about it, I knew it was something I would love. And when I come across something that feels good, I follow it."

"Just like that?"

"You bet. Anything else is a waste."

"What did you do before?"

His laugh is gentle, like his smile. "I've done a lot over the years. I'm not like you, building something massive over a long period. I've written books, experimented in different industries, and explored whatever seems like the right thing to do. It's how I like to live my life: if it feels good, follow it. It has to feel right."

"So whatever makes you happy, you just do it?"

"Oh, no. Happiness isn't always present. Discomfort is often part of the process. It's not about it always feeling 'good,'" he says, making his fingers into quotation marks. "But it has to feel right."

"What's the difference?"

"Deep down, you know it's amazing," he replies. "On the surface, you may feel scared. It may feel overwhelming and impossible, and you resist it. But deep down, you know you need to do it. If you don't, you'll regret it. I imagine you went through something similar when you first started Contollo?"

"Oh, yeah. I wanted to give up many times."

"But you didn't."

"No."

"Why?"

"I knew it was a good idea. I knew the world needed it. We're too connected these days, and the way we communicate with each other is so inefficient. I didn't know exactly how to solve it . . . I guess I still don't. But I know there's a solution."

"There you go," he says, arching his head back and looking up toward the tree. "That's the difference between something feeling good and feeling right. It's my governing force in life."

"Was it Burning Man where you learned that?"

"No," he says, still looking up. "I've always felt this way. Even at the age of five, playing with toy Ferraris, I wondered, 'What's the point?' I couldn't understand why everyone seemed obsessed with material possessions. At school, I didn't get why we would learn about math and weather and not focus on those big, existential questions."

"You must have been an interesting kid," I say.

He laughs. "Right? I think I drove everyone insane. I had a question for everything. There's always been a voice inside me, telling me to block out that noise from the media, parents, teachers, and so on. I guess everyone has that voice, but maybe mine's louder."

"That's good," I say. "I've been noticing my own voice more of late."

He nods. "It brings its own issues. I felt confused and isolated as a kid. I had a lot of angst. Everyone seemed capable of fitting in. Whereas I was always that 'one kid,' you know?" I nod. "But Burning Man did help me. It marked a huge tipping point in my life."

"How so?"

"I first went there because I felt lost. Even though I've always had this existential outlook, I still found myself caught in the hustle, like everyone in our generation seems to be."

"I wouldn't have pictured that," I say.

"Even a hippie, free-loving spirit like me." He winks. "It's the nature of this society. I didn't know it at the time. I thought I was happy. But I was so busy. I tried to be the best at everything: the best entrepreneur I could be, the fittest and healthiest person I knew, the biggest and strongest and fastest. No matter what I did, I had an obsessive approach to it. If I did something, I had to be all in, one hundred percent."

"I know that feeling."

"I'm sure you do."

"So you lost sight of what mattered?"

"I didn't just lose sight." He laughs. "I switched it off. I was always switched on to the 'thing' in front of me. If I wasn't working, I was at the gym, pushing myself to the limit. If I wasn't at the gym, I had to be learning about something, so I could be even better. I had to meet new people because, if I didn't, I might miss out. I was exhausted. Worse, I was addicted to it. In a weird way, it made me feel good."

"Like you were achieving something?"

"Exactly." He takes a deep breath. "Of course, these days, I know what I was doing."

"What?"

"Avoidance. Resistance. Too scared to face the questions I needed to, so I kept busy, pushed it all to one side."

My shoulders feel heavy, my neck sore, the air heavier, weighing me down.

"This one time, I had a date with a woman I had been flirting with for weeks," he continues. "It went great. We had a good time. We liked each other. And then, we went back to my place, and I couldn't get it up." He shakes his head. "I wanted her. She wanted me. I was young and, on the surface, at the top of the mountain. But there was more going on than I knew. I was exhausted. I was too switched on to work and everything else; I had literally forgotten how to switch it all off." He scoots closer to me, disturbing the sticks on the ground. "Because I had always been this philosophical thinker, I felt like I did everything for a good reason. I didn't do business to make a ton of money; I did it to have a massive impact. I didn't hit the gym just to build muscle; I did yoga and dance, too, so I could be fast and flexible, as well as big and strong. I ate clean. I was open-minded. I didn't follow trends. Yet the hustle is the hustle. Whatever the cause, exhaustion is what it is."

"And that's when you went to Burning Man?"

"Not long after, yeah. I found myself in a strange place. I started to think about suicide. Like a waterfall, all the feelings I'd pushed down rushed forward. I realized how stressed and sad I felt. I decided that if I didn't feel better within a year, I would end my life."

"Really?" He nods. "Wow."

"I truly believe, and always have, that the purpose of life is to have the most enriching experience possible. I'd stopped doing it. If I couldn't fix that, I didn't see the point in living."

I feel the ache within, the pressure of letting everything build up. My chest feels so tight. *How long has it felt this way? Has it been like this for years, and I didn't notice?*

"What did you do?" I ask.

"I let go. I made a promise to be less regimented. To play more. To be spontaneous and go with the flow. I wanted to find enjoyment in life again. And I did. It didn't take long to feel better. When you let the universe in like that, it often gives you what you need. It led me to Burning Man. I was like you at the time. I'd researched it and spoken to other people. It looked cool. It sounded amazing. But I didn't really get it. I didn't know what to expect." He pauses, stares into my eyes once more, leans in. "As soon as I got there, I *got* it. Seventy-five thousand people coming together and being present in the moment, open to letting in the thoughts and feelings they usually push down. It's a transcendent experience, which is why words alone will never do it justice."

I take a deep breath. The heavy ache is still there. It's always there.

"It strips you of expectation, worry, and the pressure that builds up in everyday life," he continues. "It washes over you, empties you, and refills you. It gave me permission to be who I wanted to be and opened my eyes to a lot of new experiences and opportunities."

"Like what?"

"For starters, it introduced me to the tradition of Ayahuasca. You heard of it?"

"That ritual where you drink a drug-infused tea?"

He laughs, shaking his head and placing his palms on mine. "It's much more than that, man. Yet before my first Burning Man, I would likely have said something similar. But shortly after my first burn, I went on an Ayahuasca retreat. It's the most profound experience I've ever had. I had three ceremonies over a few days, each one unique and transformational."

"Didn't you just hallucinate it all, though?"

He laughs warmly. "No. I transcended into a new realm of consciousness, connected with my higher self. The world, and how I see it, has been different ever since. Like Burning Man, words alone don't do it justice. Although I did try to share my journey as best I could; I wrote a book about it."

"Yeah?"

"Remind me when we leave. I'll get you a copy."

"Thanks. I'd like to read that. Though, I'll be honest, I think something like that is way beyond me."

"Why do you say that?"

"I'm too logical, I guess."

He laughs, lowering himself onto his back and staring up at the sky. "That is exactly why you should do it."

Two boys chase each other in front of us, dodging benches and trees. They're maybe six years old. It's been twenty years since I was that age. I imagine I ran and played like they are. If I think back and focus on the past, memories creep forward slowly, trips to the park with Mom and Dad; recess at school, with friends I've long since let go of; vacations and meeting strangers, instant friendships forming. I had a good childhood. I always had love and attention, as an only child often does. I got to go places and experience new things; I had nothing to complain about, never lacked what I needed. Yet the memories don't rush forward. They aren't just there to grab at any time I wish. I have to think and unlock my mind, push all the noise to one side. Will those two boys one day not recall this moment, as they run around, free, with huge smiles on their faces?

Will they, too—like me, like all of us, maybe—overwhelm their minds with boxes to check?

"They're so free," Michael says, leaning on the picnic table. We've moved from our tree, taken a quick stroll around the park, and ended up back where we started.

"Those kids?"

"Yeah."

I nod. "It must be nice to have that."

"What's stopping you?"

I laugh. "Life, I guess."

"No," he says, offering another gentle smile as he gazes out. "That's just an excuse. We get to choose. There's nothing stopping us from playing like that."

"So if we got up and started playing with those kids, nobody would say anything?"

He laughs. "I don't know about that. But there's nothing stopping us from getting up and playing a game of tag."

"Really?"

"What would happen?"

"I imagine we'd get a few weird looks."

"So?" he counters.

I look at them both, sprinting as fast as they can. I picture Kamal and his advice to not care about what anyone else thinks or says. "You're right. There is nothing stopping us. Except ourselves."

He snaps his fingers and sits upright. "That's right. The life we lead locks us into a default setting, full of routine and expectation. We're adults, so we should act as such. We should be mature and responsible. But the way I see it is life is a chance for us to play, whatever our age. It's a gift. It's the most amazing gift we're given, and we're only given one of them."

"True."

"You were talking about *flow* earlier, as we walked," he continues. "*Play* is an integral part of flow. When you play, nothing else matters but the moment. Look at those two kids." He points toward them. "They don't care about anything right now other than the moment they're in. They don't think about what game they will play next. They aren't worried about tomorrow or the day after. Why is that?"

"They don't have any responsibility. It's easy for them."

"True. It's easier for a kid to play. They don't have to worry about the sort of things an adult does. The expectation for a child is to play. If those two were sitting on a bench, tapping away on a laptop with a coffee in hand, we'd think they were weird."

"Yeah." I chuckle.

"We talk about flow as some unattainable aspect of life that only a few get to experience, but we've all experienced it many times before. As children, we practically lived our lives in flow, in the moment. We played. We built our entire existence around playing and doing what we wanted, when we wanted. You talk about *futures* and *presents* . . . well, as a little kid, just about everyone's a *present*. It's beautiful. It's so simple."

"Simple?"

"Yes, absolutely."

"It isn't though, is it?"

"Why?"

"Because, as you get older, your role changes. There are expectations and responsibilities. You go from being the kid to teaching the kid."

"Sure. That's a good point. But what better way to teach than to show them how it's done? We may not have as much opportunity to play like a kid does because we have a million others things to think about. We do, to extent, have to think about tomorrow and the day after, and the future. But does that mean we can't ever have time to just play? To lose ourselves in the moment and do what we want, when we want?" I say nothing. "I play every single day," he continues. "I did it this morning, before I met you. I play through dance. I've always loved it, but along the way, I lost sight of the true nature of it. I tried to master it and perfect certain moves. I did what adults tend to do, thinking about the *next thing*. But if those kids started dancing right now, would they care how good they were? Or would they move and flail their arms and look like idiots?"

I smile, tapping back into those long ago memories. I remember a time, on vacation, I think, as my parents stood to one side of the long wooden bar. Along with a few other kids, I danced a dance that nobody would ever teach. I wasn't dancing so much as throwing my body on the floor, spinning, and thrusting my arms and legs. I pulled faces and laughed and showcased ever more ridiculous moves to the kids next to me, my new best friends.

"That's how I dance each day," he says. "I have a room in my place, and it has bars and poles. I put on some music and dance. No agenda. I never have a clue what I'm going to do next. I just do whatever my body wants to. I sometimes share it on social media, and some of the comments I get . . ." He laughs. "But I love it. I feel so free. I let go of what I should be and just focus on being me, in the moment, present, in *flow*." He whips his long hair to the other side of his head. "You've just read *Stealing Fire*, right?"

"I did. It was great."

"You remember the section about 'Estasis?'"

"Yeah, I think so."

"Timelessness, effortlessness, richness, and selflessness: the building blocks of flow. When you play, you always dance between at least a couple of these. It helps you let go of everything your mind's consumed by and tap into your subconscious. That is flow. It isn't about meditation or anything like that. It can be. That works for some but not for everyone. For me, getting into flow is about doing something I love. Which is the very essence of playing, right? You just do it. Do what you want, the way you want."

"It's just that easy for you?"

"It isn't easy, no. It took me years to realize that this is my way of getting into flow. You have to find your way, and then practice it. Because it does take time. But once you get there, you stay there. I feel like I've lived inside of flow for the last five years. But I spent a lifetime before that trying to find it."

"You've spent five years in flow?"

"In essence, sure. It's not like I don't feel pain or have bad days. But when I do, I recognize it and let go. I do something that helps me tap into the moment and appreciate who I am and where I am. Is it an intense state of flow like they talk about in *Stealing Fire*? Sometimes but not always. For me, flow is just feeling present and at peace. You feel cleansed."

"Like at Burning Man?"

"Exactly. Experiencing a *burn* is an intense version of it. But each time I play, I feel rebooted and energized. I feel amazing, all because I spent a few minutes acting insane."

I smile. "You make it sound simple."

He breathes deep, in and then out. His chest moves in sync, disturbing the necklaces hung around his neck, them swaying gently side to side. "It is. You have felt it before. Many times as a kid, when you didn't care about anything other than playing and having fun. But later in life, too, with certain people who seem to halt time or activities that seem effortless. Everyone experiences it.

The problem is, most don't appreciate when they have it, so they struggle to tap into it whenever they want to."

"That's me," I say. "I know I've experienced it in the past. I just don't know how to get into that state now. I'm not sure how it feels. I can't remember it properly. It's like I'm looking for something but have no idea what it looks like." I sigh. "It's like a drunken dream."

He smiles. "You'll find it. You're already further along than most people will ever be. You're asking the questions. You're searching for the answers. Will they come when you want them to? Will they look how you want them to look? I don't know. What I do know is, once you start down this rabbit hole, there's no turning back." He pushes his hands through his hair, stretches his entire chest, and pushes it out. "Man, I wish we had this conversation a few weeks ago. I would have taken you to Burning Man. If you go there with a closed mind, you won't get it. It's just a bunch of hippies in the desert taking drugs. But if you go with an open mind, having asked the questions you've started to . . ." He sighs, a long, deep, and refreshing breath. "The curtain drops, and you get to see what you need to on the other side."

"Bad timing, huh?"

He shrugs. "Maybe. But maybe not." He smiles, more seductive now.

"What are you thinking?"

"Well, we could always catch a flight to the Amazon."

"What do you mean? Why?"

"Well, I happen to know a couple of people who are going on an Ayahuasca retreat in a few days. So the timing may be better than you think."

"No. No way, man. I'm definitely not ready for something like that."

"Why?"

"I've never done anything like it before."

"So?"

"It would be like asking me to jump in the deep end after my first swimming lesson. I've only ever smoked weed. And the whole spiritual side, and that entire world . . . it's not me. I'm only just starting to—"

He holds my hand, halts my rambling. "Sometimes in life, you need a kick to wake up. Psychedelics can be that kick when it comes to finding flow. It's how a lot of people enter the rabbit hole. But engaging with Mother Ayahuasca goes way beyond a *trip*. She shows you parts of yourself that you otherwise refuse to see. I know firsthand that you find what you're looking for. It's different for everyone. It's often painful. Yet you come through it, not only cleansed, but transformed."

I shake my head; my stomach tenses with the thought of it. "I really don't think I'm ready for something like that, Michael. I appreciate it, I do. And maybe later, in a few months or something, but—"

"Later? In a few months?" He smiles seductively again. "Come on, you know that's no way to live life. Nothing is an obligation. Everything is a choice. And this is yours. I will not push you. But if you choose to do this, I will go with you."

"You'll come? Do the ceremonies again?" He shakes his head. "Why? You'll have me do it, but you won't do it yourself? Why?"

He pauses, hangs on his thought. "I feel like I'm always with Mother Ayahuasca," he says. "Similar to how I always feel in flow, I'm in constant communication with her. Drinking it again would be unnecessary. Maybe I'll feel the need to one day, but that day isn't now." He smiles, looks into the distance. "Even though we've just met, I truly believe you need this. I see it. I know it. I would love to experience it with you. I just have no need to re-experience it for myself."

My chest thumps; I feel anxious, although, maybe, I'm excited, curious. I'm not sure. "Oh man," I say, biting my lip and rubbing my face.

TWENTY-SIX.

Wil's House, Dayton (Ohio)

"What have you discovered?" Wil asks.

"A lot," I say. "Although, at the same time, nothing."

He laughs, strokes his clean-shaven chin, and moves both hands to his knees. We're sitting in his minimalist living room—the beige walls, the same chairs in the same place, a small table separating them, the record player, the crate of vinyl next to it, the larger table, the glasses, and the bottle of whiskey. There's less in it than the last time I was here. The white statue, with its bearded face and curled hair on top, stares at me.

"Yes, yes. Indeed," he says. "It often feels like that. You feel no progress. The only constant seems to be more questions." He looks around the room. "But you know, deep down, there's growth. You can feel it, sense it. It's there, m'boy. You know it, yes?" I nod. "I can see it in you, too. You're different. Tell me. Tell me your journey."

I smile and look down at my steaming cup of coffee. My hands wrap around it, warm and tingling. I do feel the growth. I do sense that I'm different from the person I was. Or maybe, as AJ suggested at the start, I've rediscovered who I once was.

"I don't fully understand how I feel," I say. "I feel sad, I know that much. There's a heaviness within me. A strange, dull ache. I suppose, in a way, it feels like mourning."

"Of course, of course." Wil says. "You are. Mourning who you were, m'boy."

"I guess. But more than just who I was, I feel sad about what I've clung to. If I think back to how I acted when Jordan interviewed me . . ." I laugh, a gentle chuckle. "It was only a few months ago, but it seems like a lifetime. I thought so much of myself. I looked down on others." I look at Wil, catching his eye. "I thought I was better than everyone." He nods. Lifts his cup to his mouth. "Jordan put me in my place. I needed that. I needed someone to tell me, 'You're nothing special.' He forced me to open my eyes, but I was still asleep. Still not ready to see what I needed to."

"Ah, yes, there are many sleepwalkers among us. Those with open eyes but still dreaming. Who woke you, m'boy?"

"You did," I say. "Speaking to AJ is what inspired me to question things, but coming to visit you is what showed me real change was possible. I noticed how much you had grown over the last year. You, not long ago, seemed fueled by ego and money and the lifestyle we were living. But then, just like that, you didn't seem to care about any of it. I didn't appreciate it at the time, but visiting you gave me hope." He nods again, slouched in his chair. "But I was too scared to face it. It was like I had been woken up, but I lay in bed, too frightened to get out of it. In New York, when I met up with Matt and Ishita, I just felt angry and frustrated. At everything. I wanted to go back to sleep, back to how things were."

"Indeed. Easier that way."

"It wasn't until I met Kamal and we traveled east that I committed to it. I knew there was no turning back, and I knew I didn't want to. I realized how I pushed so many people away, including myself. I saw in Kamal a guy who didn't care. He seems so comfortable and at ease with who he is. I wanted that." I chuckle again. "I remembered how I used to be like that, growing up. Even a few years ago, I had that spark." I shake my head. "It was gone, and I didn't know how to get back to it. Gini tried to teach me about trust; Hollis, about resistance; Jules, about my mind, my body, and my spirit; and you, too, were there. I could intellectually understand it all, and say 'I want that,' but—"

"It's easy to say but much harder to take the steps you need to."

I nod. "Yeah." I drink from my cup, the warm coffee sliding down my throat. "I was scared. I just wanted a solution, for someone to give me the answer. I hated it. I hated that I wanted it so bad. I've never been that guy. I've always taken pride in being a person who got what I needed to get. But as I think back to Bali . . ." I shake my head again. "I was practically begging for help."

"Is there something wrong with needing that?"

"No," I say. "But I wanted someone to do it for me. I didn't want to do the work, and I guess that is when the sadness kicked in—the heaviness. I realized how I had treated people. How I had started to look down on them. How I began to think I was better than them, because I had money and success…" My words fade away as I flip my wrist in the air and sigh. "I suddenly saw how I'd treated people I once cared about. Like Christian, who had become a convenience. Keeping them around for my own gain. It's why I kept Beckie around for as long as I did. I should have broken up with her months earlier. I should have let her move on.

I wanted a girlfriend but only for show. I didn't want to actually put in the work a relationship needs." I hang my head, pay attention to the heaviness within. "I had stopped wanting to put in the hard work for anything. I was a big deal, so it should all just work out for me."

"Is the fear still there?" Wil asks.

"No," I say. "Maybe, I suppose. But not in a way that holds me back. Not like it did. It doesn't feel overwhelming anymore. It's just there now, like any other emotion."

"Marvelous news, m'boy. It's a scary thing, fear, when it grips you." I nod, my eyes heavy. "Did the Amazon rid you of this fear?"

"In a way."

"How?"

Three weeks have passed since I first met Michael. Within seventy-two hours, we were in Peru. The journey to our destination, where the Ayahuasca ceremonies took place, was an eye-opening experience in itself. Rickety boats down the Amazon River. Treks through thick jungle. Rain so intense it washed me clean. Thunder so loud it ran through me.

During our journey there, I felt uncomfortable and anxious, afraid. "I'm not sure I'm ready for this," I said to Michael, an hour before my first ceremony.

"Are you ever ready for the truth?"

Shortly after, I sat in a large tent with eight people I'd known less than three days, ready to put a hallucinogenic into my system for the first time in my life. I've drunk a lot and smoked a decent amount of weed. But no LSD or mushrooms. Nothing that came close to the substance I was about to put into my body.

Everyone else seemed ready. They all embraced this lifestyle and had lived a version of it for some time. I had no clue about any of it and was completely out of my comfort zone. I didn't want to stay. I wanted to run. It wasn't for me. I wasn't like these people. I wasn't like Michael. All this was a terrible idea, and it wouldn't help me.

Yet I knew where all these thoughts came from: fear. I was afraid, more afraid than I have ever been in my life. Not about what might happen to me and how I might feel but what I might find.

What happened next remains a blur. I cannot differentiate between what was real and what was a dream. In a way, it all seems like a nightmare. I'm not even sure I was awake for any of it. If it wasn't for the fact that I threw up, a lot, I'd be sure I fell asleep instantly and had the worst night terror of my life.

Shapes, strange figures, and whispers of colors filled me. I didn't just see them but felt them. Voices, too, not only audible but the physical feeling they were inside me. Terrified, I struggled to breathe. Sweat dripped from me, soaking my shirt. The first ceremony brought no clarity, no epiphany, nothing but a purge of sweat, vomit, and the worst diarrhea of my life.

I found no flow and no answers. But the next morning, I did feel clean, cleansed, as Michael suggested I would.

The second ceremony was harder. More intense. Less so physically, but it seemed to tear my mind apart. The same vision kept coming forward again and again. Similar to the dream I keep having yet more vivid and detailed than ever.

I climbed a mountain, the wind and snow beating against my naked body. Looking down, I saw jagged rocks and people who didn't look like people. Their faces blurred into swirling dark colors that distorting their features. They reached up to me. I sensed they were angry, wanting to hurt me. I felt them get closer, so I clung tighter and tried to climb up the rocky face. But I couldn't. Each time I did, I would fall, screaming as I dropped toward the ground and into their hands. I thought I would die. I wanted to die. But I never did. Each fall brought me back to the same place on the mountainside, stuck once more, to repeat the process. The whole experience seemed to last forever. A voice kept talking to me. "Climb. You have to climb. Let go, and you'll climb. You cannot stay here."

The voice was soft, gentle, kind—contrasting with the demonic setting I seemed trapped inside.

Eventually, the rock held firm enough that I made it onto a ledge. This ledge felt familiar, as though I'd been there before. And then the familiar feeling of having lost someone appeared. It attacked my chest, made it even harder to breathe. A sudden, intense fear ran through my entire body. I panicked as the wind crept under my clothes and chilled me to my core. I tried to shout out to them, but nothing came out. My throat, my lungs, were empty. I span in circles, unable to see or make sense of anything through the wind and rain. But then, the silhouetted figure appeared, just out of reach and along the ledge. I knew it was who I was looking for. They were just here, with me, but then they had left. They had disappeared. I loved them. I needed them. I didn't know who it was, but my feeling toward them was so intense and powerful. "You have to climb," the silhouetted figure said, its voice seeming to come from inside me. "Let go, and you'll climb. You cannot stay here. You do not belong here." I tried to reach for them and to speak once more, to tell them how I felt; that I was sorry; that I was sorry I had hurt them and pushed them away, and that I would do anything to have them come back to me. But to no avail. Nothing left my lungs, not even my breath as my chest got tighter and tighter. Nudging my feet along the narrow edge, I slipped as the rock gave way, clinging to the side of the mountain and pushing my fingers into it as hard as I could. "Let go, and you'll climb," the voice said once more. I felt so scared. So cold. So helpless, as though the end had arrived.

And then I fell, falling and falling for what seemed like eternity, eventually coming to, curled up on the floor and crying; our shaman stood over me offering his hand.

I didn't take part in the third and final ceremony. I couldn't. I shook, unable to calm my mind or my body for hours afterward. I feared Michael and our shamans would push me to.

They didn't.

"It's okay," Michael said. "You have found all you need to."

"I've found nothing," I said, tears streaming down my cheeks. "I'm broken. It broke me." He hugged me. Said nothing. I didn't feel anger toward him. I wrapped my arms around him and pulled him closer. A warm rush filled me, reminding me of long-ago memories of clinging to my mother: love, kindness, and safety.

"I don't want to talk about what I went through," I say to Wil, taking a deep breath. "I still find it hard to think about. At the time, I regretted going. It was the hardest thing I've ever gone through. I couldn't determine what was real and what was a dream. The whole experience was surreal, but in the time since, I've begun to find some peace." I shake my head. "I just can't make any sense out of it, though. It feels like it's on the tip of my tongue, but at the same time, locked away, deep in the back of my mind, and—"

"M'boy, it's okay," Wil says. "You can tell me when you're ready, or tell me never. Are you okay? Do you need a stiffer drink?"

"I'm fine." I take another deep breath and smile. "That's the strange thing. I found the whole experience terrifying, yet it does seem to have set me free. That fear . . .the strange, dull and heavy ache . . . it's still there but no longer hurts. I feel calm and at peace."

"So it did cleanse you?"

"I have no idea." I laugh. "Every time I think about it, it shakes me to my core. But I'm okay with that. I'm okay with everything, which isn't something I've felt for a long time."

He smiles, bobs his head, and taps his knees. I notice his blue eyes, light and bright like mine. I don't think I've ever noticed them before, nor the way his curly hair loops neatly around his ears rather than flopping over them. He's trimmed and neat: eyebrows, hair, even the stubble that peeks through his unbuttoned shirt. It contrasts his frantic words and how he mixes, skips, and muddles up sentences. "And what about Contollo?" He asks. "Answers, any of those there?"

I shrug my shoulders and smile. "No clue. Ray keeps messaging, trying to call me. I know I need to make a decision, and I know I'm resisting it, but . . . I don't know."

"Do you even care?"

"I do. If anything, I care more about Contollo now than I ever have. I keep thinking about the vision I had for it in the beginning. In its current form? I don't know. I'm not sure it's even possible to change things now. It's grown so big. Maybe it's grown beyond me."

"How do you feel about that?"

I shrug again. "I don't feel much. I know I should. But I'm okay. Whatever happens, it will be fine."

"M'boy, how very stoic of you." I raise my glass to him and smile. "I am proud of you," he continues. "You seem well and truly cleansed, rejuvenated and reborn. Even if it did shake you to your core."

"Michael said it would cleanse me as we traveled to Peru. I underestimated how powerful the whole experience would be. I didn't know what to expect, but I certainly didn't expect what happened." I breathe deep, slowly exhale. "I've been having this same, recurring dream over the last few months. I've not told anyone about it, but each time I've dreamt about it, it's shaken me. During the second ceremony, I went through something similar to that dream but worse than I have ever experienced. It seemed to last for hours, forever, even, but then, at the same time, it passed in a blink of an eye. I couldn't close my eyes for hours afterward, I was so afraid. But when that fear dissolved, it seemed to take something with it. It's strange, because I can't say I feel happy right now, because in truth, I am where I've been all along. I'm still lost. I have no clue what comes next. But I'm no longer unhappy. Does that even make sense?"

"Indeed it does, m'boy. A toast," Wil says, raising his cup. "And as Marcus once said, 'to accept without arrogance, to let go with indifference.'"

"Marcus Aurelius?"

"Oh, yes. The one and only." He points behind him, to the lone figure standing atop his table. "Do you know much about Stoic Philosophy?" he asks.

"I can't say I do."

He smiles that wild grin of his that lights up his entire face. "Do you recall when you were last here, how I spoke of letting go of the clutter in my life?"

I nod.

"At the time, we talked about how I let go of the *things* in my life—books, gadgets, clothes—to be minimal. But this isn't where my personal cleansing began, and in truth, it wasn't the most important part. Because before you can let go of the many things that surround you, you must first simply learn to let go." He leans closer, places his palm over his chest. "Of those thoughts, feelings, desires, fears, everything. Not always let go, in the sense of ridding them. Because if a feeling is real, it is real. But rather, letting go by accepting it is there. Letting go by letting it in, letting it *be*." He places his coffee cup on the floor and joins me on the couch. "Stoicism is a fascinating and layered subject, but in essence, it comes down to *letting go*. We have so little control in our lives, and yet most of us—all of us—commit so much energy into gaining control over the uncontrollable. It blinds us, corrupts us, and, if we let it, defines us.

"Letting go allows us to break free and simply be: be with your thoughts, be with your feelings, be who you are, and be in love with who that person is." He stops, takes a deep breath. "It sounds like your journey has given you this, given you permission to let go of what you spent years trying desperately to control."

My chest flutters—a strange tingling sensation, warm and soothing.

"You are ready, my friend."

"For what?"

"For what comes next. Whatever that may be."

TWENTY-SEVEN.

Thirty Thousand Feet Above Toronto

"I tried to kill myself," he said. "You are the only person who knows."

Wil didn't look at me. Inches from me on the same couch, he seemed to slip away into his own past.

"I told you about my friend, Dante. How he was taken from us too soon. I told you about my travels of self-sabotage and how I lived without living. I also told you about my apparent awakening, and how I traveled to the States in a bid to fulfill my destiny but once again, lost myself in a cacophony of lies, distraction, and meaningless sex and success.

"I told you of Turndog and how he helped me so much, yet only after he first turned me away for not being ready. And you have seen with your own eyes much of my progress and the person I've become: still imperfect but more rounded. Yet what I didn't tell you is that I slipped into despair one evening and gave into my weakest of weaknesses. I pushed a handful of pills into my mouth and washed them down with four glasses of scotch. I thought it would be enough. Maybe something within me knew it wouldn't be, a part of me not ready to go. Yet the conscious part of me was. I wrote the letter. I came to peace with the dark ether that awaited me. I was ready. The ultimate form of *letting go*."

"Wil," I stuttered each letter. "When? Why?"

"Shortly after moving to Dayton. I came here hoping it would give me the answers I desired. Much like you traveled and begged for answers from other people, I came here in a bid to find *it*. I'm not like you, my friend. I've only ever been able to speak, truly, to one person. He was taken from me. I suffer in silence. I try to find the words I need in here," he continued, pointing to his head. "I had reached a point where every epiphany seemed to come with the caveat of 'not quite yet.' I was nearly ready, but I wasn't quite ready. People like Turndog seemed to reinforce this. I was tired.

"Much like you have felt of late, I was sad. Sad about who I had been my entire life. Sad about who I had become since losing my best friend." He took a deep breath. "Sad about losing him. I missed him so much. I still do. But during this period, I missed him to the extent that I would speak to him when I was alone. I wanted to join him in the darkness.

"I did all I could to take my mind off of what haunted me. I surrounded myself with people. I worked relentlessly. My head ached from all the hours, and my body suffered alongside it. I had nothing left in the place that matters most." He stopped, pointed to his chest this time. "I was empty, and I reached a point where I figured that maybe it would always be like this. If that was the case, then why not end things? After all, who would truly miss me? It's not like I have a family. The pain would pass. I would be here, and then I wouldn't."

"What happened?" I whispered.

"I did it. I took the pills. I let go, in the literal sense. But then, sometime the next day, I woke up. I must have drunk too much, as I'd thrown up. A lot. I felt terribly ill and very much wanted to kill myself again due to the horrendous aftermath. But I was very much alive. And something strange happened . . . I was okay with it. Not relieved. Not happy. Just okay. I felt strangely stoic about the whole experience, and I continued to feel like this for the next few days as I sat with my thoughts.

"I wrote. I sang. I played my guitar. I went for walks. I did no work. I didn't think about what would come next. Strangest of all, I didn't think of Dante. I just thought of life, my life. What it all means." He smiled, seemed to laugh gently at something he'd said. "I came up with no answers. I didn't feel like I had gained any clarity. Yet I felt okay with that. Much like your trip to the Amazon cleansed you, my failure to kill myself seemed to cleanse me."

We sat on his couch, the room growing darker, as afternoon gave way to evening. Wil told me his tale of near-death and old stories about shedding his life of possessions, changing his direction in work, and learning about philosophy and spirituality. So much of what he said mirrored what I have felt. I heard his pain and how it had manifested into something he was no longer able to bear. He let me in. He unloaded it all on me as I sat and listened, as so many have done for me.

I stare out the window. Remnants of clouds whip past at a frightening pace. A patchwork of life rests below, as towns and cities conjoin together in neat rows and imperfect squares. When you're down there, amongst it, you cannot see. It's life: people passing you by, cars hurtling past, the hustle and bustle of work, family life, and whatever else. But up here, as you look down, it takes on a new form. The streets lead somewhere. Each road has a specific purpose. You can map out where you need to go. It spreads out toward the horizon. Beyond that, I do not know . . .

We're en route to Toronto. A guy Wil knows, Sol, is running an event. It's about cookies or something. He insisted I come. I didn't resist. I have nowhere to go, so I've decided to remain open to what comes my way, trusting it will lead somewhere.

Let go, as Wil keeps telling me.

Let go, as so many people have.

Each time I look at Wil, I feel an incredible sadness. With one or two more pills, or one fewer glass of whiskey, he might not be here. He suffered, alone and in isolation. I don't understand it. I understand the pain because I've felt it. The frustration. The confusion. The fear of fear itself and the notion of facing it. Not knowing what comes next, but knowing you have to take the leap because *this* simply is not what you want. But it hasn't sent me so low. Was that where I was heading? In time, would I, too, reach a point with nowhere else to turn but a bottle of pills and a glass of *Jack*?

"M'boy, this world we live in today is too fast," he said, sadness in his eyes. "We're always connected, always have access to how other people live. We do nothing but compare who we are to who someone else is, desperate to have what they have. Not because we want it, but because they seem to have something we do not. And maybe it's that *something* that is the reason they're happy and fulfilled and have it all *figured out*, the reason they're happier and better than we are.

"Yet we only see an edited version of their life. We don't get to see who they truly are. Nobody gets to see that but Prometheus himself." He looked at me, smiled. "During my low point, I would think of you often. I would think about how successful you were and how happy you seemed. You lived an amazing life."

I bowed my head, looked at the ground, considered my edited story, the life I not only lived within but also shared with the world.

"All along, you, too, were lost. You, Ferdinand Foy himself: human, like the rest of us. You, the guy with everything in the world, including the worries and demons we all go to bed with."

We had continued to talk deep into the night. About how business in this modern world seduces you to work so long, so hard, and so relentlessly, until you have nothing left but emptiness. The overwhelm. The stress. The bombardment of messages, people, brands, ideas, content, and temptations. These were the exact things that led me to Contollo in the first place. I planned to rid the world of the overwhelm. Yet all I can see is how we've added a great deal more.

I had figured I suffered through something few other people did. I have a massive business that weighs heavy on my shoulders. I have eyes on me from all directions. People look up to me and expect so much of me: to succeed, to be the benchmark, to have the answer. I had assumed my pain was unique, but as we spoke, I realized neither money nor fame defines this pain.

It weighs on everyone—likely always has. Yet in this modern world of connected carnage, what chance do we have?

Wil had handed me a few books and suggested I read them: *Meditations* by Marcus Aurelius, *Moral Epistles* and *Letters from a Stoic* by Seneca, and *Enchiridion* by Epictetus.

"I have never understood religion," he said. "The idea that a single deity rules over us . . . I find it absurd. Losing Dante only soured my taste, but as I sat at rock bottom, I recalled how Turndog often quoted snippets of philosophy and spirituality. At the time, I brushed it away, of course," he said, flipping his wrist. "But when you're at rock bottom, you see things differently. It's so dark down there; to let any light in, you must open your eyes wider."

I pictured the rainforest, the dark green leaves overhead. I remembered how I'd fought so hard but had no choice but to relent and give in to what my subconscious mind insisted on showing me.

"I began with this one," he said, pointing to *Meditations* by Marcus Aurelius. "Had I tried to read it a few months earlier, I sense it would have made no sense."

"But it did?"

"Oh, yes, m'boy. Each page seemed to unlock a new room inside my mind. I realized I was the opposite of a stoic person. Literally everything that defines stoicism, I am not, or, should I say, was not. In truth, none of us are naturally stoic or not. Stoicism is simply being free from the fog of life, to see what's literally in front of you and to let go of it. But life creates a haze for us all. Everything about me that wasn't stoic was simply fear, past pain, and ego. It was life, my life, warping my surroundings."

"What did you see?" I asked. "What did it unlock?"

"Everything." He smiled. "And nothing. Because, when you let go, there's not much to see. No worry. No stress or turmoil. No comparisons or guilt or the fear that you aren't achieving what you should. All of a sudden, you're sitting in an empty room. No distractions. No chaos." He smiled. "It gives you plenty of time to reflect."

"Yeah," I said, relating.

"This was the point at which I solved Turndog's little riddle, the same one I gave to you."

"Really?"

"I was ready. And because I was, he welcomed me into the [eso reo] community with open arms."

"What was it like? What did you do?" He smiled and tapped his nose. "Oh, come on."

"Soon, m'boy. I sense your time is soon. Timing is everything. No matter what the solution is, it only works if you're ready to solve the problem."

"I am ready," I said. "You said as much."

"Almost, m'boy, almost. Your time to transcend is near."

I rolled my eyes but decided to not push any further. To let go is to do just that. Let go.

I still sense the frustration. It's in there, inside me. I can't rid myself of feelings or beliefs and the ego that's so deeply rooted. It's a commitment, one I must recommit to each day. Through the good. Through the bad. With each success or failure.

The ground is near now. In a matter of minutes, we'll land. I haven't been to Toronto before. I had no need to. I have no need now. Yet here I am, trapped inside a metal capsule once more, with no control, as often is the case in life.

TWENTY-EIGHT.

Enoteca Sociale, Toronto

It's warm, pleasant. The room is dimly lit with free-hanging light bulbs above the table, shining orange. Thirteen faces surround me, none familiar except for Wil's. He knows a few people. He's talking with animated arms that become part of the stories he tells.

We're away from the rest of the restaurant, tucked away downstairs, in the cellar—a private room that Sol arranged, inviting a select few who will attend tomorrow's "cookie-off." I have no idea what that is. Wil doesn't seem to know a great deal, either. The man behind the event sits to my left, in conversation with a guy I briefly spoke to before we sat down.

The quick exchange of small talk—what you do, where you've been, where you're going—I used to excel at it. I had a locker full of pitches for each occasion. I cringe at the thought, a chilling shudder rising up my spine and across my shoulders. I close my eyes and breathe, a deep inhale. I take note of what's within: calmness, a peace I'm beginning to get used to.

Yet that queasy feeling remains, a sadness of sorts, less about my own journey and recent past, more about the general unease of the world I'm a part of. I can't shift it; my mind wanders back to what I've observed over the years with blind bliss—conversations about how hard and long we work, a contest of who wants it the most; comparing my followers and friends and connections with some stranger I've just met; the endless chatter about raising money, building teams, and launching new products.

As I've taken part in these countless conversations where I've masked my own pain, has the other person done the same? Do they, too, wear a mask, pushing themselves to feel worthy and *enough*? Do they wake up each day to a voice that wants to speak but refuse it a whisper? These people around this table, what pain do they feel? They must feel it, feel something. I see their faces, but what lies beyond them?

I've been so focused on myself that I didn't consider that maybe the rest of the world suffers alongside me: more, less, different . . .

Each time I spot a face, I wonder about their pain now. *What are they feeling? What are they keeping to themselves, scared to let anyone else know about? Are they as desperate as Wil was? Does Wil still feel that hopelessness, his mind straying off course and into those dark corners?*

You think you know. You see people—see how happy and content they are—and presume they're fine.

Maybe they are. Maybe they're not. How do you know?

I look at Wil across from me.

In the car from the airport, he broke the silence. "Ferdinand, m'boy, I keep thinking about what your friend AJ said. About going a mile deep." He rubbed his chin, looked toward the Toronto skyline. "I believe it's what I need to do. I find myself still clinging to what I *should* do. Work with this client and that . . ." He brushed his hand to one side, as if brushing away the words. "I don't enjoy it, creating art for them. I thought I did, but these last few days with you . . ." He looked at me and smiled. "I'm afraid to do what I need to."

"What's that?" I asked.

"I have no idea." He laughed, punching me gently on the arm. "I'll never go a mile deep doing what I'm doing. Make money? Yes. Get fame? Maybe. Be in demand and have my ego stroked? Of course. But I often think about what Dante would say." He cleared his throat. "He would be proud of me, I have no doubt. The fact that I'm doing something, anything with my life . . . he'd be happy for me. But he always believed with such intensity that I needed to get what's in here out into the world," he continued, pointing at his forehead. "I believe I am scared to share that. Actually, no. I *am* scared. I know it is true. You have helped me realize this, m'boy. Thank you."

"You're thanking me?" I laughed.

"You have done more than you know, my friend." He looked back out toward Toronto. "Far more, far more."

We haven't said much since, checking into our hotel and getting ready for this dinner. As one of the last to arrive, the owner accompanied us downstairs and introduced us to the group. Wil and Sol hugged, laughing and joking. I made my introductions, chatting and sharing brief stories as my mind whistled within, full of thoughts and memories of dinners just like this, comparing who I was to who I am now.

Different, yet not.

"How are you doing, Ferdinand?" Sol asks, nudging my arm and setting me free from my internal wandering.

"Good. It's a nice setup you have."

"Thanks. The main event's tomorrow, but I like this one as much." He looks around the table, smiles. "You've been to Toronto before, right?"

"Nope. First time."

"Really? How're you finding it?"

"Haven't seen much. Came straight here." My turn to look around the table. "It's a great room. You host dinners like this often?"

"I've done a few here, and I try to arrange dinners like this as often as I can. I usually do them when I travel to a new city. I find it's a great way to meet people but also to connect those I know with each other."

I nod and stare at the shelves filled with bottles of wine and decanters. Rich, dark wood touches every surface of this room, in unison with the dark, yet soothing, ambience. I turn my attention back to Sol, another set of brown eyes so much richer and darker than my own. Flicks of grey disturb his black hair, even more grey filling his thick yet immaculately kept beard. "That's cool," I say. "And thanks for having me, too. I know I was a last minute addition. Hope it didn't throw off your plans."

"Nah. Happy to have you. And if you need any help with where to go in the city, let me know."

"Thanks." I take a deep breath, looking across the table at the various plates filled with cookies. "So what is it with you and cookies? I've never known anyone dedicate an entire event to them. Aren't you a nutritionist as well?"

He laughs. "Kind of. I run *Examine.com*, which dives into the science behind nutrition and supplements. We don't have too many articles on eating cookies, that's for sure. But what can I say? I love them. And, honestly, I don't know how it's gotten so big. Tomorrow's event is going to be insane."

"Wil said over a hundred people are coming."

"Yeah. They've all paid $500 to eat cookies. Pretty crazy, huh?"

"I'd say. You've done a few of these?"

"Yeah. I had a huge sweet tooth as a kid. I was a big kid, too. I lost weight as I got older, but the sweet tooth remained. Me and cookies . . . what can I say? We're on good terms. And here in Toronto," he puffs out his cheeks and continues, "there are some amazing cookies."

"Yeah?"

He nods. "That's how it all started. Whenever I had a meeting or would catch up with someone, I'd take them to some place that made amazing cookies. I got to know the owners and became known as the 'cookie guy' amongst my friends. After a while, we started to run these small blind-taste events. It was crazy. People I barely knew would ask me if they could come to the next one. So I decided to do a charity event and invited whoever wanted to come. I figured it would be a bust, but we raised $850. It blew my mind."

"So, what? You turned it into a business after that?"

"No way. This is no business. I just thought it was fun. I asked myself, 'How crazy can we make this?' There was no goal or plan. We just did a few other cookie events and then decided to take it to New York. In Toronto, it's easy. I know all the places and people I need to. But, in New York, I hardly know anyone." He shrugs. "I thought 'screw it.' I jacked up the price of the tickets to $250 each and sold out in a few weeks. We raised $25,000 for that one."

"$25,000 from cookies?"

"Yep. We sold out tomorrow's in a few days. I think we'll raise close to $100,000."

I snort a breath and raise my glass. "That's impressive."

He raises his glass to mine. “Thanks. It’s been fun. I have no idea how tomorrow will go, but I’m sure it will be fine.”

“I’m sure it will.” I laugh. “I’ll be honest, I had no idea what I was coming to. But it sounds like it will be fun.” I grab a cookie from the plate nearest to me. “So what’s next? You going to start a cookie brand or something?”

“Nah. I think this will be the last one. I’ll do a few small events maybe, but no more *cookie-offs*.”

“How come? Sounds like you’ve just built momentum. Now’s the time to double down, surely.”

He smiles. “You would think. But I have no need for it. Once you start monetizing something, there’s an expectation. At the moment, I’m just the ‘cookie guy’ who runs weird events. Nobody expects anything from me. I don’t want the added responsibility.”

“I guess—” I say, biting off a chunk of cookie, the sweet taste of chocolate instantly playing with my taste buds. “But still, isn’t there a part of you that wants to see how successful you can make it?”

He shrugs. “Not really. For me, success is being able to do what I want, when I want. The more responsibility I have, the less opportunity I have to do that. I’m always looking to get rid of things in my life, not add to it.”

“I can see why you’re friends with Wil,” I say, picturing his minimal house and recent transformation.

“Plus, right now, these events are all about the people who come. Like these dinners, they’re a chance to connect folk. There’s no expectation or sale. Which is a break for everyone around this table because they’re caught up in business each day. Coming to a dinner like this allows them to unwind and break free. It’s amazing to see.”

"I like that," I say, considering the thoughts and questions roaming inside my mind once again. "And I guess if you don't need to do this for the money, there's no point."

"Exactly. If you have no money, you need to monetize your skills and relationships. It's just how it is. But once you reach that threshold where you don't have to worry about it, the fewer responsibilities you have, the better."

"I'm starting to see that," I say, finishing off my cookie. "This is delicious, by the way."

"It's good, right?" He smiles, almost hidden in his beard, and takes one for himself. "Wil said you've taken some time away from Contollo. How's that gone?"

"Honestly, it's been a roller coaster. If you'd said all of that to me a few months ago, I would have thought you were crazy. But now, I'm starting to realize there's more to life than building the biggest business you can."

"Yeah. I love business, and I love money. I wouldn't be able to live the life I do without it. But there comes a point when you start to want more of it just for the sake of it. I think everyone goes through that."

"Did you?"

"Sure."

"How did you escape it?"

"I don't think there was any one thing. I went through a rough patch at twenty-three, which humbled me. But I think what's really helped me over the years is staying friends with people I grew up with. Take this room," he says, motioning around the table. "There's some serious talent in here, but they offer you a completely warped sense of reality. We all have more money than most people do, and we all have the freedom to walk away for a few weeks or take a day off whenever we please." He raises an eyebrow.

"You're in the middle of a sabbatical that's taken you around the world, right?"

"Yeah."

"Most people can't do that. They have a nine-to-five and a budget. That's the situation most of my old friends are in. So I'd invite them to do something random like go rally racing on a Wednesday. I'd call them up and they'd say, 'Sol, I can't just take Wednesday off. And I don't have a spare $1,500 lying around.' That kind of thing humbles you. Reminds you what's going on in the world. It grounds you."

I bite my lip and rub my chin. "Yeah. I can't say I have any friends like that anymore."

"They help you remember what matters most," he continues. "Not money or how successful the world thinks you are. I love those guys I grew up with. I didn't want to lose them from my life. Sure, sometimes I involve them in *this* world. I have season tickets for the Raptors, for instance, and I invite them along to games. But sometimes we just go and grab a drink in a dive bar. It doesn't matter, as long as I'm around the people I like."

I grab another cookie, hold it to my nose—fresh, as delicious to smell as it is to taste. "It's a good outlook to have."

"It's easy to lose yourself in it all," he continues, puffing out his cheeks. "Truth is, most entrepreneurs become so self-absorbed. Not because they're selfish but because they get stuck in a bubble where you want more and more so you can match the lifestyle everyone else is living." He smiles. "You end up creating a random event for kicks but then think about how you can scale it and make a bunch of money for yourself." He looks at me, winks.

"Touché."

"It's not just about doing what you want, when you want either," he continues, "but getting to involve other people in it, whether they live in *this* world or not." He bites into his cookie. "Can I make other people happy while I have fun myself? Can I do what I want to do but make it about other people? I find it's a lot more fun that way."

I wipe my face, rubbing the five-day-old stubble up and down. I focus within, search my memory for the last time I had a meal or drink with a friend from my past—someone without a business, who doesn't live and breathe Silicon Valley, who's responsible for paying their bills each month, and consciously thinks about each penny that comes and goes.

Even on this trip, the only people I've met have lived in *this* world, one that affords them the freedom to do what they want, when they want. I close my eyes, feel the ache within, the sadness. I still don't understand it.

What are you trying to tell me?

I sigh. Maybe Wil is right; maybe I'm not ready yet. I still cling to a life I no longer want, pushing it out of arm's reach but not out of sight. The same way I've treated Christian, and Beckie, and everyone else—a sense of knowing what to do but no conviction to do it.

TWENTY-NINE.

Outside of Enoteca Sociale, Toronto

There's a chill in the air, a stronger breeze than I'm used to. The seasons are changing. The warmth of summer coming to an end, the crispness of fall fast approaching. I recall the sticky heat of the Amazon. It feels both near and far—trees replaced with buildings, the noise of nature drowned out by the rush of human life: sirens, engines, shouts, and more.

I bundle my arms across my chest to keep in the heat.

The meal continues inside, but I needed to get outside and breathe a little. Surrounding myself with others doesn't seem as necessary now. Being on my own does. That ache continues, the questions and wonderings with it.

I think of Wil, how he wants to go deeper and no longer skim the surface but remains afraid to commit to that, to change his direction once more. He resists. His art is so incredible; he shouldn't. He will be fine. He will be more than fine. I know it, and I sense he does, deep down. But the fear—it has a hold on him.

The same fear has a hold of me.

I know what I have to do. I must let go. It's time for me to change course because the path Contollo is on is not the one I want. I'm desperate to miss it, to wake up in the morning and yearn to go back—to the company I created, the family I built. My baby.

But I don't. I do not miss it. Not what it's become.

Allowing these honest thoughts in hurts. Part of me fights back, resists it. *No. Don't let it in.* Maybe this is why the heavy ache feels so heavy. It trembles up my throat, to my nose, and then my eyes, stinging, heavy with the truth. I must let go, move on, but . . . how?

I close my eyes and hold a deep breath of chilled air in my lungs. I think of my conversation with Sol, how my mind immediately navigated toward more—*more money, more events, more fame from his cookie curiosity*. How he'd looked at me, almost with pity.

I don't want to be that guy, obsessed with money and market share.

I don't want to be the guy who creates a vision, only to forget about it.

But I am. I am that guy, and I will continue to be as long as Contollo continues on its path.

Yet am I able to change its course? Is it not bigger than me, already moving beyond me? Ray has already told me as much, before this entire adventure began. It isn't my baby anymore, and it stopped being mine the moment I invited one silver-haired man in after another. They brought money and experience with them, but with it, an insistence of a certain direction that we must travel toward. They convinced me it was the right way. I convinced myself it was the right way. Deep down, I guess it never sat well with me. That voice tried to make me listen, yet I drowned it out with anything I could find to distract me from the truth.

In the same way I haven't missed Contollo or what it's become, I sense it hasn't missed me. It continues to make money, for me and the board. But what about the customer? What about going a mile deep with them? It doesn't matter anymore. It's no longer part of the plan, and that plan is happening with or without me.

I open my eyes, watch Toronto pass me by. My eyes glisten, chilled in this nighttime air.

I picture the mountain from my drug-induced state, how I clung to the side of it so tightly, unable to move. The silhouetted figure, just out of reach, how it told me to *climb. You must climb. Let go, and you'll climb. You cannot stay here.*

Fear consumed me. *I cannot let go. If I let go, I will fall,* I thought. Yet the tighter I gripped the more rock broke free, until I had nothing left to cling to, falling . . . falling . . . falling into the arms of the faceless men that sat in the abyss below.

"Let go, and you'll climb," the voice said. I focus on the heavy ache within, it still present. *Let go*. Everything is telling me to, but how?

"You needed to get some air too, huh?" Sol asks, standing alongside me.

I wipe my eyes with my hands. "Yeah. It's warm in there. Although it's getting cold out here. Not used to it." My heart races.

He holds his hands to his mouth, blows in them. "Not much cold where you've traveled recently. What's next for you?"

"Good question," I say.

He nods, gazing out toward the streets, seeming to take it all in. "It's good to take a break. Can be tough to know when to get back into it, though."

"Tell me about it." I smile. "This is the first time I've taken anything resembling a break in . . . I don't even know. Maybe five years. Part of me is ready to get back, but another part—"

"Never wants to return?" he steps in, laughing.

"Something like that." I take a deep breath in, the chill tingling against my tongue. "I've always been a very decisive person. Had a plan. Can see what comes next. And when I can't see it, I take the time to figure out the solution."

"Not so easy this time?"

I shake my head. "What's strange is, I'm okay with it."

"Well, it will all work out for you, I'm sure."

"Yeah. I sense I have some tough decisions to make soon."

"You ready to make them?"

"Yes. And no." He laughs, blows into his hands once more. "I think Contollo and I need to break up," I say with a long exhale. I surprise myself. The words just come out.

"Really?"

"Yeah."

"Big step."

My eyes widen. "We're not on the same path anymore. I don't know if it's evolved that way or been pushed by other people. Either way, I guess it doesn't matter."

"It happens," he says, nonchalantly. "When it does, it usually opens up new opportunities."

"Yeah. But letting go . . . it's hard."

"It is."

I cup my hands and blow into them. Instant warmth, brief and fading. "Adulting is hard."

"Maybe," he says. "But not really. We have the freedom to do what we want. I like to look at having that responsibility as a good thing. If we didn't have it, well, that's no world I want to live in."

"True," I say. "True."

"Why do you feel you and Contollo have to break up, if you don't mind me asking?"

"I set out to change how we communicate with each other. For a while, I truly believed we were doing that. We were building something great. But these days, we're part of the problem more than anything. Adding to it, rather than removing it."

"Why do you say that?"

"All we do is add more features that look cool but don't actually do anything. It does nothing but feed people's unnecessary desires and tops up their endorphins. Little, fleeting spikes of happiness." I close my eyes and shake my head. "We skim the surface, but the plan was to go a mile deep—evolve how we communicate, not create more white noise."

"And you don't think you could get back to that?"

"With Contollo? I don't think so. The board would dismiss it."

"Have you proposed it to them?"

"No." He says nothing, a slight smile drawing across his face as he watches the streets of Toronto thrive in the night. I shake my head and stifle a laugh. "I guess I'm still living in a black-and-white world," I say to myself.

"Maybe you can right the course," Sol says. "Maybe not. Either way, it's a journey. You don't have to have all the answers. It's not like Contollo was this massive empire in the beginning, right? I imagine, at the start, you just had fun with it. Let what be, be."

"Yeah," I say, smiling. "I'd like those days back."

"You have new days to create. Just have fun with it again. Let it evolve. In time, you'll look back and see the progress. Like I said inside, I have no idea how everything has led to tomorrow's event. It blows my mind. There's no way I could have imagined any of this in the beginning. I couldn't have planned for it if I wanted to. But it happened. And I truly believe it's because I had zero expectations, minimal responsibility, and just had fun along the way."

He places his hand on my shoulder. "Anyway, I better head back in. See you inside?"

"Yeah. I won't be long." I close my eyes and allow the street's orchestra to consume me. The noise of everything blurs into nothing. I retreat within.

I love you. I love you. I. Love. You.

I take note of how I feel. The ache is not as intense, barely noticeable, in fact. It's as though voicing what I was afraid to admit released a valve. My insides deflate, becoming lighter and lighter.

Maybe *letting go* doesn't mean I have to let go of Contollo, but rather, let go of who I was, who I've become: a CEO, an authority, a founder, a man at the helm, leading everyone else below. At the top, I'm handcuffed, unable to find a solution to the problem I need to solve. But if I was free to roam beneath, under the radar and away from the expectations that have weighed me down, free of the responsibility to lead everyone and everything, a chance to just have fun and enjoy the moment, to find *flow* . . .

I open my eyes. I feel a tear, then a second. That ache is no more. I feel light, so light I could float.

Let go, and you'll climb.

I understand the voice. I understand the ache that's weighed me down. I think I've always understood. I just didn't want to. I understand my drug-induced vision and what Mother Ayahuasca wanted to show me, why I clung to the mountainside so tight it hurt. I needed to let go of it. To loosen my grip and allow the very forces I fought so hard to take control and help me ascend up the cliff's face. The longer I resisted and clung tightly, the more painful my fall, hurtling toward those men with no faces. I know, too, the person I searched for in my dream, the one I had lost and who had left me, the dark silhouette just out of reach. It was me, my spirit, that inner voice pleading with me to let go. "You don't belong here," it said. "You cannot stay here. Let go, and you'll climb." It's been guiding me all this time, throughout the day as I drown it out, and then at night as it's given its chance to speak.

"I am not a CEO," I whisper into the chilled, night air.

I am not Contollo.

Contollo is not me.

I am free to be me.

More tears escape, rolling down my cheek and chilling my skin. I think of Wil and something he said: "Your time to transcend is near." Michael had said something similar. To transcend is to go beyond, to push through and past the barriers I've set for myself. "I'm not a CEO," I whisper again. "I must let go." I smile. More tears follow. That heavy ache, it wasn't there to hurt me but rather to guide me. to help me transcend.

Transcendence . . .

I laugh, thinking of Wil once more. I pull out my phone and shake my head. "Transcendence," I say. Opening my browser, I type: esoreo.com. I press *enter* and let it load.

To enter this site, you must literally climb beyond the summit.

I tap my keyboard; the clickity-clack of fake keys barely audible over the hustle and bustle of the busy streets. *Transcendence.* I press *enter* once more. The white screen disappears and a new one loads with large letters that spell out: *Welcome, friend.*

The End of Part 1

The journey began with *Beyond The Pale.*
It continues with Part 2: *Beyond The Horizon.*
To read the opening of this installment,
visit: beyondbook.co/horizon

YOU NOW KNOW HOW TO ENTER

WWW.ESOREO.COM

Explore the [eso reo] experience and discover how to go beyond your own pale.

If this book has helped open your eyes, what happens next will help you ascend.

ABOUT THE AUTHOR

Matthew Turner is a British author who lives in a small town in Yorkshire, England. Having previously published three novels and a non-fiction business book, he wrote *Beyond The Pale* on the back of interviewing hundreds of successful entrepreneurs, authors, investors, and thought-leaders. Gaining a unique insight into areas such as mindset, flow, and personal development, and gaining a reputation for crafting compelling stories out of other peoples' lives, Matthew builds relatable fables for those looking to live a meaningful and purpose-driven life.

As well as writing for himself, Matthew ghostwrites both articles and books for other successful entrepreneurs and thought-leaders, between spending time with his two children.

If you enjoyed this book, please leave an honest review on Amazon, Goodreads, or your preferred online retailer.

For more information, visit: beyondbook.co/horizon

CPSIA information can be obtained
at www.ICGtesting.com
Printed in the USA
JSHW021935170723
44903JS00002B/336